OUTLAW TALES
of Alaska

True Stories of the Last Frontier's Most Infamous Crooks, Culprits, and Cutthroats

John W. Heaton

TWODOT

GUILFORD, CONNECTICUT
HELENA, MONTANA
AN IMPRINT OF GLOBE PEQUOT PRESS

To buy books in quantity for corporate use
or incentives, call **(800) 962-0973**
or e-mail **premiums@GlobePequot.com**.

A · TWODOT® · BOOK

Project editor: David Legere
Map © 2010 Morris Book Publishing, LLC

Library of Congress Cataloging-in-Publication Data is available on file.

ISBN 978-0-7627-5326-0

Printed in the United States of America

10 9 8 7 6 5 4 3 2 1

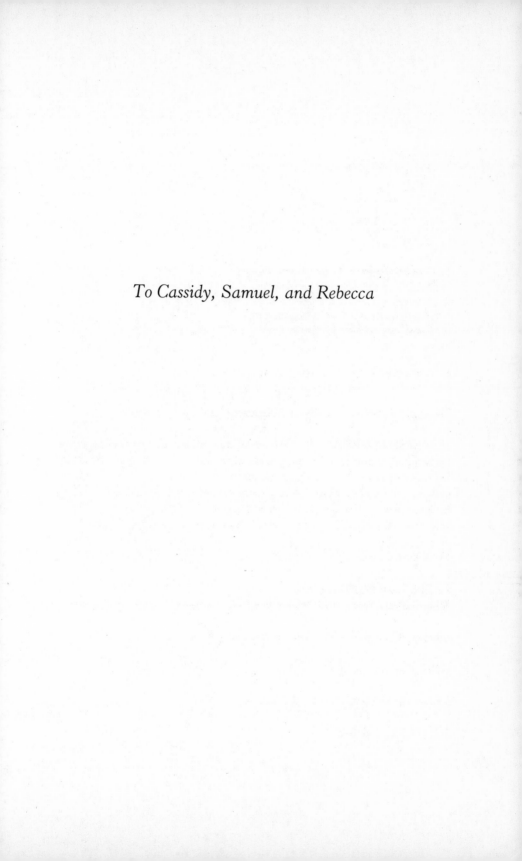

To Cassidy, Samuel, and Rebecca

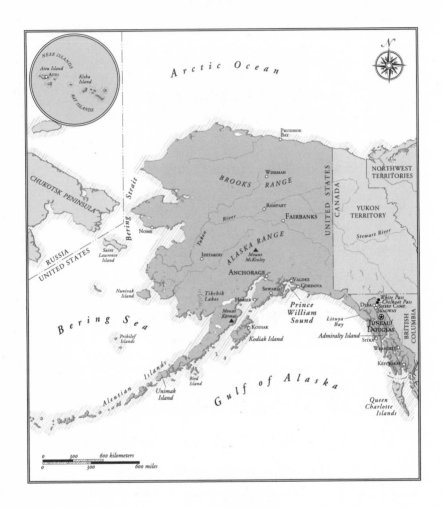

ALASKA

Contents

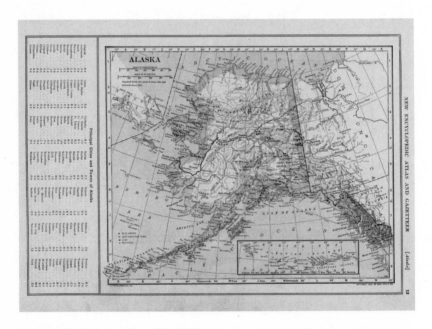

A map of Alaska produced in 1907. *Rare Maps Collection, G4370 1907 D6. Archives. Alaska and Polar Regions Collections. Rasmuson Library, University of Alaska, Fairbanks.*

Introduction

Alaska represents many things to many people. When Johnny Horton sang Mike Phillips's famous song "North to Alaska" in 1960, he captured the essence of the popular "Last Frontier" sentiment that strongly influenced Americans during the early Cold War era. The song invoked the gold rush glory days, heroic races to the gold fields of the northern frontier, majestic peaks and untamed rivers, the northern lights, and the loneliness of isolated prospectors. It celebrated the hardships, determination, and success of an exceptional people and way of life. The hero of the song, Sam McCord, was indeed a "mighty man," played by John Wayne in the movie that shared the same title as the theme song. The hero had to be strong because he went up against a bad outlaw who sought to steal not only the fruits of his labor, but his girl as well.

This hit movie tapped a national mood. The story of Alaska represented no less than the last chapter of the mythical rise and expansion of American civilization across the continent. Phillips's song and Wayne's character referenced many key ideals that Americans cherished: grit, epic struggle, adventure, and destiny. Alaska, for many Americans, *was* the Last Frontier, the last chance for a people to tame a wilderness and experience a cultural and spiritual regeneration in the process. All obstacles to progress, including the nefarious deeds of larger-than-life northern outlaws, must be overcome in the grand pageant of American history.

Such a view helps explain our collective fascination with outlaw stories. America produces heroes with the strength to overcome even the "baddest" outlaws. We may not have practical proof to substantiate this cultural view of the past, but in the mythical rendering of our national story, such a truth has always been self-evident. Americans see themselves as an exceptional people—Alaskans see themselves as even more exceptional!

Professional historians today might argue that this mythical last frontier was not the exceptional place that most Alaskan residents today believe it was. Indeed, for many people "outside" of Alaska, the forty-ninth state represents instead the "Last Wilderness," a place to be preserved and experienced, not a frontier to be exploited. But these interpretations, debated by scholars and true believers either from a distance or from the relative comfort of their modern homes and conveniences, more often than not reflect their partisan political and intellectual persuasions, or personal identities. Such views can obscure the lived realities of the individual characters that experienced the rugged life in Alaska around the turn of the twentieth century.

For the men and women who went north to Alaska in the late nineteenth and early twentieth centuries, their real experiences were personal and imbued with a private meaning. Historians and chroniclers can only try to re-create their experiences and ascribe meaning to them. When I agreed to take on this book project, my decision was based in part on a desire to divert my attention from the more heavy scholarly efforts that I was engaged in. I thought the project sounded interesting, fun, and entertaining. This thought proved correct, but I unexpectedly discovered that constructing the vignettes of Alaska outlaws for this volume provided an intriguing lens through which to consider the early history of Alaska. These were fascinating characters whose criminal exploits created situations that required a social response. The interplay between outlaws and law-abiding citizens tells us much about a society and culture. These stories underscore the view of Americans as a boisterous, energetic, and restless people more than a century ago.

True to this series, the following pages provide overviews of a nasty cast of Alaskan frontier characters. The lives of these Alaskans were shaped by the remoteness of the territory as well as the vastness and variability of its geography and the extremes of weather, sunlight, and darkness. These natural elements tested Alaskans' endurance in ways that differed from the western American experience elsewhere. Some held up better than others under the strain. A varied population of mobile and transient adventurers thronged to the North Country beginning in the late nineteenth century to join an already diverse indigenous population. The chapters of this book explore the exploits of some of the worst elements of this populace, but in the process the broader outlines of life in the Territory emerge.

Charles Hendrickson:
The Blue Parka Bandit

One would not ordinarily consider Fairbanks, Alaska, to be a desert environment, but the Alaskan Interior receives only about fifteen inches of precipitation annually. It also can get quite warm during the summer. In June 1905, on one of these hot Interior Alaska days, an old man came into Fairbanks from the north trail. The mosquitoes molested him fiercely as he tramped across the bridge into the boomtown. Not too many men were on the streets, but the dazed old man stopped the first passerby he saw to announce that he had just been held up, by the Blue Parka Bandit! This news quickly spread through the dirt streets. Men streamed out of saloons, stores, and tents to learn more. There had recently been a string of holdups that spring, and people were on edge. As they crowded around the old man to get the details, he simply said that the bandit did not take any of his money; rather, he had given the old man money to buy a drink, and that is exactly what he intended to do! There was some laughter and a few grunts of disbelief, but the crowd was now intrigued, and probed him for more of the story.

The old man, a little defensive now, sipped on his drink and recounted his story. He had been coming down the trail from Pedro Dome where it wound through the woods. As he hiked through a thick spruce stand the Blue Parka Bandit suddenly appeared on the trail. The old man did not notice him until he heard the bandit tell him to give him his gold. Startled, the old man looked up and saw the man's steely eyes and a rifle resting like a baby in his big arms. He reflexively complied and reached into his pocket for his poke without resistance or complaint. The big man in the blue parka seemed an intimidating figure of authority at that moment. Compliance came naturally. As the old man considered his predicament, his heart began to race. In an instant, he had lost control of his own destiny to a man in a blue parka carrying a .30-30 rifle! The old man tossed his money over to the bandit. Within seconds the highwayman realized that there was only ten dollars to be had from this traveler. The bandit chuckled and asked if there was anything else of value in the old man's pockets. The old man said that was all he had on him. Having a rifle barrel pointed straight at your heart acts like a truth serum. The bandit knew the old-timer spoke without guile. So, he returned the money to the poke, threw it to the old man, and instructed him to put it back in his pocket. Then, to the consternation and maybe even admiration of everyone listening to the story, the Blue Parka Bandit reached into his own pocket, pulled out some coins, and tossed them to the old man. He told the old-timer to buy himself a drink when he got to the next saloon. Then he stepped back into the trees and vanished.

Fairbanks, Alaska, is located in the geographic center of the state. This fact, coupled with its historical significance as a major gold-mining center in the Far North, resulted in residents declaring their city to be the Golden Heart of Alaska. The city sits against the backdrop of the Tanana Hills in the north, a cluster of rolling hills that do not reach more than 2,000 feet in elevation. Follow the streets leading south long enough and one reaches the Tanana Flats, a wide valley draining the river of that name. These muskeg flats, notoriously boggy and mosquito-infested in the summer and frozen solid in the winter, stretch for about 50 miles or so until they connect with the Alaska Range. Denali, or Mount McKinley, the tallest mountain in North America, is the most significant mountain in this spectacular range. A small river, the Chena, meanders through the town on its way to the confluence with the mighty Tanana River 10 miles below Fairbanks. The Tanana flows several hundred more miles until it feeds the more famous Yukon River. These rivers were crucial for the Athabascan Indians who lived in this region of the vast Alaskan Interior, but they also served as early transportation routes taken by military explorers and later by entrepreneurs, fur trappers, and gold seekers. Initially, all traffic into Fairbanks, founded in 1902 after the discovery of gold in the vicinity, came on these rivers.

By 1905, Fairbanks was at the height of its initial gold rush boom. About six thousand claims had been filed on the rivers and creeks of the surrounding hills. These claims produced $6 million in 1905 and $9 million the following year. The production of gold, of course, did not go unnoticed. As word spread, there was a clamor outside of the Interior to get to Fairbanks and to the diggings. There were also calls in Fairbanks to make that happen with more efficiency. The boosters in the business community wanted more and better transportation infrastructure and services to facilitate the expected growth, to lower the cost of shipping, and to improve profit margins for service industries that hoped to "mine" the miners. The initial trail through Circle City to the north and east linked Fairbanks to the Yukon River and to the Canadian Yukon Territory. It was adequate initially, and boasted roadhouses about every

20 miles that provided lodging, food, and services year-round. Nevertheless, local boosters demanded the development of an all-American route. These calls were inspired in part by nationalism, but also by a desire to remove the restraints placed on travelers and entrepreneurs by the Canadian government.

During the summer, new shallow draft boats began to ply the waters of the Tanana and the Chena. They came up the Yukon from the American side, but when the rivers froze up, people remained dependent on the Canadian route. With the rivers ice-free for only a few months out of the year, it seemed that future growth and American pride required the development of a network of trails into the Interior that started on the American side. Soon, the Valdez trail was developed. Initially, it was nothing more than a winter dogsled path that ran from Valdez, Alaska, up through the Alaska Range to the Tanana River at Delta Junction. From there it followed the river on its northern and western course above the Alaska Range and into Fairbanks. Soon, regular horse-drawn sledges and stagecoaches began to run the trail on a regular schedule of about every ten days. Roadhouses emerged along the way, and workers improved the trail until it could be called a road. Fairbanks now had regular mail service and access to the "Outside" year-round. The military also constructed a telegraph line at this time to link the military posts and the civilian communities to the Lower 47. Fairbanks emerged as a thriving outpost of civilization in the middle of the Alaskan wilderness. Along with that new civilized status, however, came thieves.

By 1905, an estimated 5,000 people lived in Fairbanks and perhaps as many as 3,000 in nearby Chena or along the creeks. The residents hailed from all over America and across the globe. This was a corporate mining town. Most of the good gold lay buried deep near bedrock. There were some surface or placer mining opportunities, but the big money in gold required big money in capital investment. As a result, Fairbanks grew quickly from a tent city to one comprised of wood cabins and frame homes, with wives and children, schools and religious and cultural institutions. There were elements of the raucous boomtown and tent-city atmosphere present in places like Dawson, but Fairbanks tried hard to present itself as a legitimate city of law and order. It suffered its share of problems, including lawlessness, vice, and gambling, but up until 1905, it remained free of highway robbery.

In fact, highwaymen seemed an exception rather than a rule in Alaska, unlike other regions of the American West. One reason for this stemmed from the lack of development. Outlaws required places to hide out and places to get away to, and Alaska offered few of these. It was too cold in the winter, too swampy and buggy in the summer, and too unpopulated all year-round. Only a few communities existed at the turn of the century in a remote region much larger than Texas. Known criminals found it hard to hide in small camps and towns where everyone knew each other and strangers stood out. In addition, they struggled with survival alone in a trackless wilderness. Then one must consider the travel distances faced during a "getaway." These distances left even the hard-core daunted at any time of year, let alone in the middle of winter. Finally, bankers or merchants grubstaked most men in the Far North. This meant that few men possessed anything other than credit in their pockets for most of the year. Once the ice on the rivers broke up and the ground thawed in late May, things changed.

Activity on the rivers and creeks and in the hydraulic mines increased, and the pokes of gold dust and nuggets that men carried began to bulge. During a four-month frenzy of activity, as long as the midnight sun continued to shine, men worked around the clock to claw at the earth in hopes that it might relinquish its riches.

At times, the amount of gold in the sluice buckets was so rich that the miners could not allow themselves to sleep. More gold begot more feverish efforts to dig, wash, and sluice. In the late spring of 1905, men working their own claims on the creeks outside of town began making their way along the trails and roads to cash in their gold, pay off debts, buy supplies, and drink. Everyone was bringing in the pay dirt and happily spending their money in Fairbanks and Chena. This was the first year in the Interior that an individual could actually make highway robbery a paying proposition. This was the Far North, and someone seized the opportunity to take advantage of the local prosperity. A few weeks into the 1905 season, reports started coming in about men being held up along the trails and roads leading into Fairbanks and Chena.

The creeks that provided the most gold to placer miners, Cleary Creek and Fairbanks Creek, were about 25 miles outside of Fairbanks to the north. To get into town from these locations, one took a trail that led up and over Cleary Summit and then down into town about 20 miles away. Up on high there were a series of rock outcroppings that gave a man a perfect view of the trail coming up from either side. An enterprising thief might spend his time well by scouting out the trails and laying in ambush for travelers on this busy route. By May, the trouble on the trails reached a crisis, with many locals afraid to travel in small parties outside of Fairbanks. The robberies were becoming a regular part of life in the region. Little information about the highwaymen could be given to the authorities because the bandits were always masked and the victims always too frightened by the experience to give a useful description of the perpetrators. Over time, though, a pattern appeared. One highwayman stood out. He was a large, powerfully built man with blond hair. He wore a blue parka and always carried a .30-30 caliber Savage rifle. His victims described him as calm, cool, maybe even professional in his approach to highway robbery. In time, he gained notoriety and came to be known as the Blue Parka Bandit or the Blue Parka Man.

The most popular story told of the Blue Parka Bandit pertained to the holdup of the Episcopalian bishop, Peter Trimble Rowe. One day in the summer of 1905, Rowe took the stagecoach out of Fairbanks, heading north with six companions. The horses toiled up Cleary Summit. The Bandit easily surprised the stage at the summit when the fatigued horses eased their pace after the hard climb. He called to the men in the coach and, with rifle trained on them, demanded that each one hand over their poke. All of the frightened men, save the bishop, complied. Rowe demanded to know the meaning of the holdup. He wanted to know how any man could have the audacity to rob one of God's ministers? Rowe told the Blue Parka Bandit his name. In one version of the story, the Bandit was said to have chuckled, saying, "Why, damn it all, Bishop, I'm a member of your congregation." He then tossed the heaviest poke to the bishop for a donation to the church before disappearing into the tree line.

In the other version of the story, the Bandit demanded money from the group. But, when the bishop revealed his identity, the Bandit pointed his rifle at the traveling partners and told them to hand their pokes over to the bishop. After each of them complied, the Bandit informed the men that they had just made a donation to the church! Then he escaped into the fog.

As these stories circulated throughout the Interior, the Blue Parka Bandit began to enjoy legendary status. Some Alaskans compared him to Robin Hood because he only helped himself to the money of rich travelers. Local merchants and businessmen, however, shared no such sentiment. They either lost money directly to the Bandit, or indirectly in terms of the diminished purchasing power of his victims. Influential voices in Fairbanks, among them the Episcopalian circuit rider Hudson Stuck, demanded action. Stuck famously traveled in a dogsled as the minister to Natives in their villages on the Yukon and Tanana rivers. His voice lent authority to the community's organization of a vigilance committee tasked with the capture of the Blue Parka Bandit. However, the deputy marshal of Fairbanks, George Dreibelbis, quickly ended this effort. He warned the editor of the local paper, who also supported the idea that anyone implicated in vigilante activity would be held accountable. Dreibelbis, a capable law enforcement officer with experience in Montana's range wars, refused to put up with any extralegal mischief.

While the vigilance movement died quickly, the community did take action approved by the constituted authority. Local businessmen organized armed "treasure trains" to move large quantities of gold shipments to and from Fairbanks. The Blue Parka Bandit thought twice about taking on twenty or more armed men guarding gold pulled from the local creeks every week. He never did try to rob one of these trains, but the daily

D. T. Kennedy's pack train with 1200 pounds of gold dust for First National Bank Fairbanks, Second shipment season 1906. *Albert Johnson Photograph Collection, 1905-1917, 1989-166-45. Archives. Alaska and Polar Regions Collections. Rasmuson Library, University of Alaska, Fairbanks.*

holdups on individuals and small groups continued into the late spring and early summer of 1905. The local paper printed the news of these holdups almost every day, and hounded the recently appointed and increasingly exasperated marshal, George Perry.

The Blue Parka Bandit began to hit closer than ever to Fairbanks. On June 16, he held up two freight drovers called Norman Campbell and Mr. Heel. Just 10 miles from Fairbanks, and nearly within view of the Gilmore Roadhouse, the Bandit surprised the two men while they were taking a breather at the top of a steep grade. When they turned to chat, the Bandit stepped up behind them, calmly presented his weapon, and with only a few words, acquired their pokes, worth about $230 altogether. He then told the men to drive on and keep their heads turned to the road. If they looked back, it would be the last thing they ever saw. The Bandit then vanished into the spruce trees. Incredibly, other drovers plied the same trail that day just a short distance in front and behind the two men held up by the Bandit. It was a bold robbery committed in full daylight on a busy road.

Just ten days later, the Bandit robbed four men just 2 miles outside of Fairbanks, near the Owl Roadhouse to the east of town. The following day, the Bandit attempted to hold up a stage. The driver, called Tommy White, managed to get away by urging his team to a full gallop before the Bandit could get him within the sights of his rifle. White made it safely to the Costa Roadhouse and elicited the help of its owner, Harry King, and a few miners in the area. They spent the rest of the day beating the brush, but found nothing. Things got so bad that the *Seattle Times* carried a shocking headline warning that bandits threatened the people of Fairbanks and the gold from the Tanana district. On June 27, an event lent credence to that headline when the Blue Parka Bandit held up Lee St. James, a traveler on the road outside of Fairbanks. St. James refused to hand over his gold without a fight. The Bandit responded to this resistance by shooting St. James before he retreated into the tree line. St. James thanked his lucky stars that day for the silver dollar that he kept in his vest pocket that deflected the Bandit's bullet. Stunned by the impact, St. James rested on the side of the road until other travelers came to his assistance.

This latest incident set off a debate in the community between the local paper and the marshal's office and one faction of Fairbanks that feared a large gang of bandits was trying to shake down the entire region, and another faction now rooting for a lone man taking on "the system." This latter group viewed the town hysteria as a source of humor, and they poked fun at their frightened neighbors. The marshal's office seemed inert at best and petrified at worst. Marshal Perry put out statements suggesting that he did not possess the resources necessary to take on this challenge. The Fairbanks *Evening News,* in disgust, took out an ad asking for donations to create a reward for the capture of the Bandit. Contributors donated $1,000 to this fund.

But then, at the height of the debate, a summer surge of rain combined with unusually hot temperatures that melted the glaciers in the Alaska Range caused flooding in Fairbanks and the low-lying areas of the Tanana Valley. Everyone scrambled to save what they could of their property and to head for high ground. When the rains abated and the waters receded by about mid-July, news spread of the recent arrest of a man for highway robbery. Fairbanksans realized that the robberies had stopped; all of the incidents had indeed been the work of one man. Local authorities made the arrest on July 11 and only released the name of the suspect, Charles Hendrickson. The alleged identity of the Bandit shocked locals, who knew Hendrickson as an amiable man, liked by all who knew him, especially women. Many who knew him best wondered how it was that he found the time to be such an active criminal. A hardworking man, Hendrickson must have rarely slept.

In the midmorning of July 11, Hendrickson had gone to the N.C. Company store to make a purchase. For some reason, the clerk had a hunch when he saw Hendrickson. He alerted the marshal that he thought the Blue Parka Bandit was in his store. Marshal Perry, desperate to close the case, decided to act on this hunch. Hendrickson became suspicious when the clerk did not return. So, he left the store and headed down to Third Street. There, the deputy marshal and his assistant contacted Hendrickson. This understated arrest seemed unbefitting to a notorious frontier outlaw. But the deputies got the drop on Hendrickson, so he cooperated—at least initially. When Dreibelbis put Hendrickson in jail without any drama, it merely marked the end of one phase of the story. The next phase pitted the wily and resourceful Hendrickson against the fearless and persistent Dreibelbis. The stage was being set for an epic battle of wits and endurance that eventually spanned vast sections of the Alaskan wilderness.

The trial started a few days later, with the Territorial prosecutor charging Hendrickson with highway robbery. Spectators in the courtroom supported Hendrickson, and circulated rumors questioning the veracity of the Territory's witnesses. The prosecution fanned these rumors with its fantastic tale that implicated Hendrickson as the point man of a vast conspiracy to rob the Interior's rich of their gold. In return for the support of coconspirators, Hendrickson shared the bounty of his illicit efforts. On this count the jury found Hendrickson not guilty, and the court erupted with cheers.

But Hendrickson did not go free.

The prosecutor felt the sting of this setback. He quickly pressed new charges against Hendrickson, who remained in custody pending the outcome of the next case against him. This time the Territory charged him with obtaining money under false pretense. The prosecutor faced the same problem in presenting this second case. All of the evidence against the defendant was circumstantial—there was no direct evidence that identified Hendrickson as the Blue Parka Bandit (except for the fact that the robberies on the roads and trails to Fairbanks had ceased since Hendrickson had been incarcerated). Even though the prosecutor could use this fact to support his case, Hendrickson was probably going to win acquittal.

Why then did Hendrickson attempt to escape the Fairbanks jail? He has been described as a paradox: the highly educated geologist with a graduate degree who chose a life of crime; a man with a work ethic that would please John Calvin, but who nonetheless preferred to gamble on his freedom; a man well liked by many people who chose the solitude of life on the run; a thief with a flair for generosity; the dangerous criminal who charmed those around him. On August 8, hours before the start of his second trial, Hendrickson sawed his way through the logs of his cell wall with a makeshift tool. No one ever learned how he acquired the tools used to make his escape. Some suggested that an accomplice slipped them in through the moss chinking that insulated the log jail.

On the morning after his escape, Hendrickson was seen by two men near the Owl Roadhouse outside of Fairbanks. The men did not realize his identity until they arrived in Fairbanks sometime later. They noted that he was carrying a .30-30 rifle that looked like it had just been removed from its box—shiny and new. Dreibelbis put together a posse and was only a few hours behind Hendrickson, but the escaped prisoner had too much of a head start, and the posse lost his trail. They returned to town defeated, at least for the moment. Fear on the trails and roads replaced the fun and excitement produced by the trial. No one doubted that Hendrickson, the Blue Parka

Bandit, would resume his old ways, or that he would fight going back to jail.

They were wrong on both counts.

Dreibelbis bided his time. He knew that he had the advantage. August is a rainy month in the Alaskan Interior. The rain softens the spongy muskeg, making it difficult to travel off trails and roads. And while the mosquitoes begin to abate because the nighttime temperatures drop, the conditions favor biting gnats that leave welts that burn and itch interminably. Winter was coming, and Dreibelbis implemented his plan. The battle was personal now. The vast scale of the Yukon-Tanana drainage drives men to seek out human company. Dreibelbis knew that he only needed to be patient and vigilant. News would surface about Hendrickson's whereabouts. Everybody in the Interior had heard about the arrest, trial, and escape. The Blue Parka Bandit was no longer an anonymous figure; someone would see him and report back.

On September 23, Dreibelbis got news that Hendrickson's cache had been discovered by chance. In October, Dreibelbis learned that Hendrickson had forced himself on three caribou hunters in their cabin during a stormy night. After helping himself to dinner, regaling his involuntary hosts with stories and humor, and spending a night sleeping on their floor, Hendrickson went on his way in the morning. It appeared that he was holed up somewhere in the Birch Creek district. The winter of 1905–06 was famously cold; temperatures dropped in late October to 60 degrees below zero.

In late October, Dreibelbis linked up with Frank Wiseman, the deputy of Cleary City, to make his move. The two men traveled by dogsled to Birch Creek in bitter cold weather. After a few mishaps, including a close call on the frozen river they traveled on, the two lawmen caught Hendrickson on Birch Creek, where he was cutting firewood for wages. Not wanting to take any chances, the two pushed back to Fairbanks with their fugitive at a deadly pace. They figured that it would be safest to push Hendrickson so hard that he would be too exhausted to attempt an escape. For seven days and nights they pushed on as the 60-below temperatures held the Interior firmly in an icy grip. By the time they made it back to Fairbanks, a grudging respect had developed between the captive and his captors because of the hardships they had endured together. Hendrickson rested peacefully, if fitfully, in the Fairbanks jail once again, as he recovered from the ordeal.

Then, in November, he got a new cellmate named Thomas Thornton, and seemed to come back to life. Thornton had been arrested for stealing a horse in August at Fort Gibbon on the Yukon River, near its confluence with the Tanana. He soon escaped and was later caught near the Canadian border at Eagle, Alaska. Now Dreibelbis had two escape artists to contend with, and he was not taking any chances. Extra men were hired to keep watch on the inmates, but it did not take long for Hendrickson and his new sidekick to make another escape. On January 29, 1906, Thornton threw pepper into the eyes of one jailer while he was being served breakfast. Hendrickson stormed through the open cell door to lunge at the other jailer. He hit him twice and put him out cold on the floor. Thornton struggled with the first guard. He finally pulled a knife that he had somehow acquired and stabbed his opponent twice near the heart and once in the back. This guard would barely survive his wounds.

It was a bitterly cold dark morning with temperatures hovering around 50 below. None of the other men being held in the jail tried to escape even though a path was now cleared. Only a fool would go out in this kind of weather. Hendrickson had grabbed a parka, but was unarmed. Word of the escape spread, and dog-team posses organized by Dreibelbis quickly set out down every trail leaving Fairbanks. Hendrickson headed out of town on the trail to Valdez, but for some reason, he apparently failed to meet up with his accomplice because he was not properly attired for the cold weather. He only made it 12 miles before he stumbled into a deserted cabin. There was no stove. One of the posses found him there a few hours later, curled up in the corner and shaking violently in the extreme cold.

Once Hendrickson was back in jail, the guards had to fend off an unruly lynch mob that gathered in the morning darkness. The severe wounding of the guard by Thornton had destroyed Hendrickson's community support. Hendrickson survived the mob and was clapped in leg irons. Dreibelbis placed him under constant watch by heavily armed guards, along with Thornton, who was caught in March. In August, Hendrickson was tried. When he appeared in court he wore "Oregon boots," circular iron weights about thirty pounds each that fit around the ankles. Thornton and Hendrickson both got fifteen years for the assault committed during their escape attempt. The Territorial government dropped all other charges to save on expenses of a longer trial.

Hendrickson was shipped out on the steamer *Lavelle Young* on September 24, with three other prisoners, including Thornton, under armed guards led by Frank Wiseman. Both Thornton and Hendrickson wore Oregon boots. Indomitable to the end, Hendrickson managed to get his hands on a jeweler's tool. He used it to fashion a key for the boots and a saw out of a brass curtain rod. When the boat stopped to take on wood, at Nation City, the convicts staged their escape plan. As their dimwitted guard daydreamed, they snuck out of the room and hopped off the boat. It took several minutes before the guard sounded an alarm.

Nation City was a gold-mining town. Hendrickson planned to get clothing and supplies from the miners. Unfortunately for him, Wiseman quickly spread the word of the escape and offered a $250 reward. Soon, everyone in the district, including a nearby Indian village, was on the lookout for the escapees. This left the runaways in a tight spot, and forced them to choose between risk of detection and capture by miners or living off the land. If the first alternative offered a recipe for disaster, the second one seemed about as bad. Neither man was prepared to survive in the bush with freezing temperatures and the threat of snow. There was nothing but a few berries left to eat out in the bush.

As desperation set in, the two partners in escape busted into a roadhouse, took supplies and winter gear, and, in effect, tipped off authorities as to their location. Next, they headed for the Canadian border, but both men had been confined for so long in irons that they were in no shape for a long overland journey.

Thornton gave up first at a roadhouse, but Hendrickson continued on to Canada. He came to a river crossing and forced the boatman to ferry him across, but the boatman seized the advantage when Hendrickson got careless. He held him until Wiseman arrived to pick him up. Finally, Wiseman got Hendrickson on the ship that would take him through the

Inside Passage down to the prison on McNeil Island. He was well known as an escape artist by the time he arrived there, and the warden was not taking any chances. And yet, Hendrickson managed to escape once more after two months on the island! He was caught before he could get off the island. This time, he was sent to Leavenworth, the maximum-security prison for the hardest cases. Hendrickson escaped two times from Leavenworth, but was caught both times after short periods on the lamb. He finally got out legally in 1920.

After that, Hendrickson fades from the historical record.

The Discoverer

During the 1890s, a Canadian pathfinder and explorer of great renown called William Ogilvie sojourned in the Yukon Territory. During his travels he gathered information about the North's geography, its Native peoples, and the colorful characters who rushed to the gold fields from the United States and elsewhere. He published much of what he learned in a guidebook about the Klondike that was widely read. He came to realize that a deep connection existed between the Americans and the Canadians who ventured north. A common cause and culture bound these men together in the Land of the Midnight Sun. Nationalism gave way in the North to ties of an "arctic brotherhood." One of the basic bonds in the Klondike mining camps that connected civilized men grew out of a self-interested effort to maintain community protection against the unscrupulous and the pathological. Numerous tales exist of frontier justice carried out against greedy or violent individuals who broke the code.

Of the many tales that he heard about and witnessed, Ogilvie recalled one that stood out because of its complexity. He recounted this story without revealing the names of the main characters, out of a quaint respect for their privacy that seems quite foreign to modern media sensibilities. Maybe Ogilvie also recognized that it was a hard case for the miners to decide, one in which the guilt and innocence of the main figures remained difficult to prove. Perhaps it was more sporting to protect their names.

This story does not provide a simple tale of right and wrong. Rather, it underscores the complexity of life on the frontier and the strong human instinct of self-preservation. I will leave it up to you, the reader, to judge the miners' decision.

The central figure of the story was a man Ogilvie called "the Discoverer." He spent the winter of 1885–86 working in Seattle, that gateway to Alaska and the Far North country. Anyone who spent much time down near the waterfront district during that period was bound to come across exotic characters recently returned from adventures in Alaska or the Yukon. That such men were prone to exaggeration was a given. Something about the rugged life of the frontiersman tended to attract the type of man given to inflating the truth and the heroic nature of their experiences with the wilderness and Native peoples. It was part of the dominant masculine culture of the North American frontier that as a greenhorn slowly evolved into a sourdough, he naturally acquired a storehouse of personal tales that, when recounted, embodied the white male identity and values. The cumulative outcome of their yarn spinning affected the next group of greenhorns to trek north. The stories conditioned their expectations, experiences, and reactions to what they saw and found in their own journeys. It was a process at once self-perpetuating and evolutionary.

As the Discoverer spent the winter in Seattle rubbing shoulders with the rugged men who fled the gold fields to go south for the winter, he began to acquire a storehouse of geographical and cultural knowledge about the Klondike, and what he took to be legitimate information about the exact location of a great gold strike. He grew more excited about this prospect each time he told the tale to those willing to listen. Such was the conviction of his words that the Discoverer eventually convinced four intrepid men, only one of whom had experience in placer mining, to partner up with him. He regaled them with details about the location, the contours of the country, the disposition of the rivers, and what to expect in that region. The Discoverer was a strong persuader. He convinced the Intrepid Four to grubstake the venture.

The Discoverer and the Intrepid Four headed out of Seattle in the spring of 1886, filled with great expectations of the riches waiting for them. The prospectors had caught the kind of fever that clouds a man's better judgment, risking all they possessed on the word of a greenhorn. But then, very few prospectors ventured into the Yukon prior to the stampede of 1897.

They booked passage on a ship that took them through Queen Charlotte Sound to the little town of Dyea, Alaska. Built along the banks of the Taiya River, Dyea would soon be in competition with Skagway, located 10 miles south, for the business of the stampeders of '98. Boosters in both communities proclaimed that their towns provided access to the most practicable routes to trailheads that led to Chilkoot Pass and White Pass, the two access routes through the Coastal Mountain Range. Skagway had the advantage of a deep harbor which made the town more accessible to ship traffic, but Dyea was located much closer to the Chilkoot Trail, the preferred pass for prospectors heading into the Klondike district. The scene at Dyea on the beach was as chaotic as it was colorful. Men who went by boat to this trailhead town were dropped off on the beach and left to scramble to get hundreds of pounds of gear and supplies to high ground before the tide came in. There were mainly tents and only a few buildings; the beach

on the high ground was often a chaotic mass of men and stacks
of wooden boxes and canvas sacks of flour, sugar, and other
commodities.

Once prospectors made it to Dyea they faced several predictable hardships. First, the men packed their gear up and
over Chilkoot Pass. The Chilkoot Trail is 3,500 feet above sea
level at its highest altitude and stretches for 33 miles. The Discoverer's intrepid party packed all of their gear over the pass
on their backs. This was no easy task. Once accomplished, it
was downhill to Lake Bennett. There they had to build their
own boats to float their gear down to the Yukon River. Once
they made the Yukon, it was a relatively easy trek down to
the Stewart River, a 300-mile tributary with headwaters in the
Mackenzie Mountains in the Central Yukon Territory region.
Upon reaching the Stewart, the party struggled against the
current to find the spot that the Discoverer had told them
about in such compelling terms. There they would find their
fortunes in gold.

After many weeks of hardship and effort, fueled mainly
by gold fever, the mining party began to cast about for signs
that they were nearing the place spoken of in Seattle by the
Discoverer's acquaintances. They had traveled up the Stewart
about as far as the directions called for, so they began to pan
for gold in all the locations that matched the description. They
found a few grains and nuggets here and there, enough to make
the work pay, but no bonanza. Certainly they expected more.
Other prospectors in the district were making a decent day's
wage for their efforts, but the Discoverer and the Intrepid Four
sought the bonanza strike, the mother lode. All their work was
supposed to be rewarded by a find that would make them

wealthy beyond their wildest dreams. The dream captivated them through the season, each nugget they found hinting at the riches soon to come.

Soon, though, as the season ebbed away, the party realized they were running short on supplies, it was too late to leave, and they needed to work quickly to put together a stake to get them through the winter. They needed about $2,500, and they needed it fast. They settled down on a claim that seemed promising and got to serious work bringing in the pay dirt. In a short time they made enough to get through the winter, and they built a cabin just as the ice came in and forced them to shut down their operations until spring breakup. After months of travel, adventure, and backbreaking effort, all was suddenly quiet and white with snow. Now there was little else to do save stoke the woodstove, eat, sleep, hunt, and wait for the sun to return to the far North Country.

The prospectors, used to activity fueled by lust for untold riches, were suddenly idle. In this inactive state, the morale of the Intrepid Four began to flag. Boredom set in, and over time, the cold and darkness coupled with confinement in a small cabin took its toll. Familiarity bred contempt. Four of the five had been friends before the beginning of the long journey, and in this situation the Discoverer became a "fifth wheel." Save one exception, none of the men had ever been prospectors. Expectations for the group were unjustifiably high. By any reasonable standard of measurement, the miners had fared relatively well. They were bringing in pay dirt, had grubstaked themselves through the winter, and were poised to make a modest income in the spring. But the Discoverer had raised their expectations to an unreasonably high level.

As the tedium grew, one of the Intrepid Four, an extremely large man known only as the "Giant" in Ogilvie's telling of the story, became disagreeable company. He began to resent the Discoverer, and convinced his friends that a trick had been played on them to pay for the Discoverer's passage up to the diggings. The Giant suggested that his compatriots join with him in exacting a little payback from the one who had criminally misled them. They had followed the Discoverer, paid his way along with theirs, dug and panned everywhere he suggested, and yet they were not rich as he had led them to believe they would be by this time. Perhaps the Discoverer was a victim too, of some deception or horrible joke played on him by a sourdough with a sick sense of humor, but, the Giant speculated, it didn't seem likely. No; it was probably a gimmick the Discoverer had devised, using the four friends to get into the gold fields himself, without any expense. Over a period of several weeks, the Intrepid Four came to a consensus. None of them were happy with their situation. None of them felt that their expectations had been fulfilled. Now there was nothing left to do but come to an agreement on what should be done about their predicament, and how to pay back the Discoverer.

Up the Stewart River there were no constituted authorities; only the miners' code pertained. Most miners in the area headed down to the mouth of the Stewart, located a few hundred miles south of Dawson on the Yukon River. So, the Intrepid Four felt completely isolated and cut off from the laws of the Territory.

If the Intrepid Four felt isolated, one can well imagine the thoughts careening around in the Discoverer's head. Outnumbered, he kept his own counsel when he heard the others discussing their dissatisfaction with the state of affairs. The Giant, more than any other member of the party, was outspoken in his desire to get revenge on the Discoverer. As the long winter dragged on, cabin fever began to set in, tempers grew short, and thought processes became compromised by the stress and strain of their conditions. The Giant's disgust and anger measurably increased, as did the severity of the punishments he suggested. Eventually, he crossed the line of propriety and fairness when he broached the idea of stringing the Discoverer up to a tree. The Intrepid Four were slowly turning into a lynch mob. The hapless Discoverer had to eat, sleep, and live with his would-be executioners. What went on in his mind cannot be minimized, as he began to fear for his life. Although the rest of the Intrepid Four did not all verbally consent to the Giant's suggestions, the topic did become a source of gallows humor. Moreover, they certainly did nothing to dissuade the Giant from such talk. Their lack of pressure to control the excesses of the Giant's intemperate comments played on the mind of the outnumbered Discoverer.

Cabin fever, the legendary malady of the Far North, is not a sickness in the physical sense. Rather, it is a symptom of a mental disorder that many people suffer in a variety of locations. Living in a small cabin is not a prerequisite for contracting the disorder, but confinement for long periods of time with other people has been known to create some psychological stress in humans. The symptoms include irritability, restlessness, sleeping excessively, and having trouble remembering things. Add to these symptoms another mental condition common in the North, seasonal affective disorder, and you have the makings for a tragedy. People with SAD sleep too much and feel lethargic and depressed. This malady usually occurs in the winter months because of a lack of exposure to sunlight. The further north one goes, the fewer hours of daylight one sees.

The Discoverer was already nervous in temperament and prone to allowing his imagination to get the better of him. He was a worrier placed, perhaps, in the worst of conditions: a dark, winter environment, living in close quarters with four men who were upset with him. It was a recipe for trouble.

As the winter months dragged on, this combination of cabin fever and SAD began to cloud the thinking of all five of the men, especially the Discoverer. He grew increasingly paranoid that the other men meant to do him in.

The Discoverer's depression-addled brain stopped thinking clearly. He formulated a plan to kill the other members of the party. It was either him or them, he concluded. The question was, how would he do it? He thought about it constantly, day and night. He could try to shoot them all, but he might only be able to pick off one or two before the others could react and perhaps kill him. A knife presented the same complications, only worse. Besides, it was too intimate a way to end the lives of so many men, and he feared he did not have the strength and intestinal fortitude to carry out such a plan. No, there had to be another way to get them all simultaneously without raising their suspicion.

Then, he hit upon a plan. Each of the men took turns cooking for a week to break up the monotony of their repasts, and to share the chore. Outside the cabin, buried in the snow, the party kept a jar of arsenic, just in case bears or other predators threatened. The Discoverer realized it would be easy to mix the poison into a pot of beans and feed it to the Intrepid Four. He waited nervously for his turn to cook. At last it came. He chose to implement his plan on a day in which the Intrepid Four went out for a day's hunting. While they were gone, the Discoverer hurriedly grabbed the arsenic from outside and mixed a very large dose of the poison, along with a chunk of bacon grease, into the pot of beans. He placed the poisonous pot onto the stove to cook for the day, and then he waited. He knew his partners would be famished when they returned. All that was left to do was wait, which was easier said than done. After an excruciatingly long day, he heard the hunting party returning to the cabin.

The Intrepid Four, tired and hungry from their day of hunting in the snow, sat down and heartily dug into the deadly repast. They noticed right off a distinct and unflattering flavor in what otherwise looked like a fine pot of pork and beans. The Discoverer, not knowing what constituted a fatal dose of arsenic, had been liberal in his application of this deadly seasoning to the pot of beans. The men began to ask why the beans tasted so foul. The Discoverer racked his brain for what seemed like an eternity. Finally, he spit out a story of how he had spilt all of the salt on the top of the red-hot stove. He could not save any of it from being singed by the heat of the stove, but he thought he could still use it, if he added more than he would have ordinarily. So, it hadn't worked out the way he'd thought it would, and he agreed that the beans tasted a little funny. The men were all hungry, so they choked down the meal; they had no reason to suspect that they had been poisoned . . . yet.

Fortunately for the Intrepid Four, their appetites had been as large as the great outdoors. They had eaten heartily of the specially "seasoned" beans. In fact, they had ingested so much

A typical miners' meeting held in October of 1898 in the Alaskan Interior.
Alaska State Library, Claude Hobert Photograph Collection, P425-6-23.

arsenic, it was not too long after they had finished their meal that they all felt an uncompromising urge to run outside in the snow and purge themselves of the poisonous pork and beans! The Discoverer had not eaten anything. He claimed that he had eaten earlier and was no longer hungry. Still, having watched the gastronomical circus going on outside the cabin, he felt constrained to feign illness lest the others grow suspicious. He made himself puke alongside the others.

Later, after nightfall, the four were sick near to death. The pains they felt in their digestive tract were truly horrific, made all the worse by the fact that there was no help anywhere for hundreds of miles. The next day, having survived, the Intrepid Four were content to simply lie in bed and take solace in having survived the night and the worst pain they had ever known. Later that evening, however, their strength began to return. They talked among themselves and wondered why their cook had not seemed to suffer as much as they had. One partner, especially, thought that the Discoverer was faking illness. He kept watch on the Discoverer to see if he might catch him in his act. This was no small task, because all four of the men suffered lingering fatigue from their ordeal. Still, the watcher fought the urge to slip into slumber. As midnight approached, the Discoverer, who had been pretending to sleep, at last satisfied himself that the Intrepid Four had all fallen into a deep slumber. He slowly sat up in his bed, slipped the blankets off his shaking body, and tried to noiselessly slide across the cabin floor toward the corner of the room. Unbeknownst to him, the watcher had been alerted by his movements in the faint light of the fireplace. The watcher became fully alert, but still acted as though he were sleeping. He saw out of one eye that the Discoverer had picked up a Winchester rifle. As the Discoverer slowly cocked the rifle and started to point it at one of the sleeping men, the watcher sprang from his bed and jumped on him. The Discoverer had been caught off guard. He got one round off, but it was a wild shot. Instantly, the other three men jumped from their slumber. When they saw the two men locked in mortal combat, they instinctively knew what was amiss. They ran to the aid of their sickly friend and helped him to disarm and apprehend the Discoverer.

A wave of panic had overcome the Discoverer. He had been found out, his plan had unraveled, and he was at the mercy of men who wanted to kill him. They bound him while the watcher described how he had kept a suspicious eye out, and his evolving theory about the origin of their sickness. Confronted with overwhelming evidence, the other three agreed with the watcher. Their partner had tried to poison them, and when that had failed, he had attempted to shoot them in their sleep. What a low-down, cowardly, conniving act. It was time to exact some payback. But, what fate should they mete out to the dastardly Discoverer? They decided to wait for sunrise to begin to ponder that question. They double-checked the bonds that held back their murderous partner and then turned in to get some much-needed sleep.

When the morning came, the four men looked in the snow in front of the cabin for the bottle of arsenic. There it was, right where it had been left in the autumn. Upon checking the contents, however, the Intrepid Four noted that it was obviously reduced in volume. Irrefutable proof of the poisoning was at hand now. A discussion ensued, and the Intrepid Four decided that they had better handle this situation cautiously. They decided they would put the matter before the entire mining camp down at the mouth of the river; it would be left up to frontier justice according to the rule of a camp majority. All agreed. That way there could be no recriminations against them for taking the law into their own hands.

Only one problem, though: The camp was about 60 miles away down the river, and they were all still too weak to travel. They agreed to continue their convalescence until all were feeling up to the trek. Eventually, they made their way downriver with their captive. Once they arrived, the members of the camp sent out word to outliers to come in for an important meeting. The code of the mining camp prevailed, and miners from the district heeded the call to participate in the deliberations. Both parties were given a chance to tell their version of events. The Intrepid Four told their tale of deception, hard travel, and hard work coming to naught. They told of searching in vain for the great strike promised to them by the Discoverer. Finally, they told of their decision to winter over and give it one more try in the spring, and how that decision had nearly cost them their lives.

Then, the Discoverer told his story. He claimed to have acted in good faith; he did indeed get the information about the claim from returning prospectors in Seattle. He believed these men and took them at their word. He sought out help from the Intrepid Four and was willing to share in the profits on an equal basis. He had no way of knowing that the information he'd been given was inaccurate, or he would not have come to the Stewart River country. He found out along with his partners that they had embarked on a wild goose chase. The Discoverer told the assemblage how the arrival of winter seemed to change the tone in their camp. The others abused him as the butt of jokes that grew more vile and foreboding. The Discoverer recounted how the Giant had threatened him with bodily harm, and later, with death. Faced with the lynch-mob mentality of his partners, he lived in constant fear of death. He resolved to kill the Intrepid Four in self-defense. The Discoverer viewed his plan as a justifiable preemptive act. It was him or them, so he chose survival. Who here in the miners' camp would do differently, he asked.

There was a ring of truth and sincerity to what the Discoverer had said. Moreover, the miners in the camp were moved by his emotional appeal. They accepted his statements as fact, along with his plea of self-defense. So compelling was his testimony that a few of the Intrepid Four were forced to admit to its veracity. They even conceded that, placed in the Discoverer's position, they probably would have done the same. They sheepishly admitted that they had failed to diffuse the tension generated by the Giant's invective-laden speeches against their partner. In their defense, they said they had not realized the extent to which the Discoverer had grown fearful of the Giant's threats.

In the end, the miners concluded that the Discoverer had acted in self-defense. Still, the camp expressed uneasiness with the Discoverer's response. Perhaps he had overreacted. It was not a black-and-white case. At the very least, the miners wanted the Discoverer to leave the district and never come back. They told him that he was not welcome in their company. They provided him with a dogsled, supplies, and a warning to stay 150 miles away from the district. If they ever saw him near the camp again, they would shoot him on sight.

That suited the Discoverer just fine; he had had his fill of the gold fields. He quickly headed up the Yukon to take the Chilkoot Pass to Dyea. He wasted no time, even though it was tough going in the bad spring weather. Along the way he stopped at Haines Junction for a much-needed rest and to get supplies. He happened to meet William Ogilvie, and it was here that the Canadian first learned of this tale. Later, as he headed down the Yukon, Ogilvie ran into some of the miners who had participated in the Discoverer's hearing. He eventually met two of the men who had been poisoned by the Discoverer, as well. They all told a similar story, and two of the Intrepid Four mentioned that they no longer blamed the Discoverer for his act, even though they also believed he had been justly banished from the district.

Indeed, most of the miners apparently believed the Discoverer would never make it out at that time of the season. In effect, they thought they had found a way to render a death sentence through banishment. Their method allowed for the ultimate punishment without guilt or consequences. It certainly represented a tough call. Was this a case of justice denied or justice served? Frontier justice indeed!

Fred Hardy

Outside the Territorial courthouse at Unalaska, an island in the Aleutians, the wind blew hard as it typically did. A storm appeared imminent. This weather seemed to match Owen Jackson's emotional state as he took the stand as the Territory's key witness in a murder trial. Jackson no doubt would have preferred to make the memories of the events on June 6 and 7, 1901, go away, but he knew that they never would. And now he sought vengeance for his murdered friends. When John McGinn, the prosecuting attorney, asked him to recount those fateful days, Jackson's face trembled slightly as he began to tell the harrowing story.

It was a late morning when Jackson and his partners, P. J. Rooney and the brothers Con and Florence Sullivan, arrived at Cape Lapin on Unimak Island, the largest island in the Aleutian Chain and located in the eastern portion of the archipelago. It had been one of those rare clear and calm mornings in this island chain known as the "cradle of the storms." In this volatile archipelago, warm currents and winds from the Pacific Ocean slam head on with the icy waters and winds of the Bering Sea.

Prospectors in this district of Alaska made a special commitment when they tried their luck here; stormy weather occurred year-round, and the islands experienced few fog- or precipitation-free days. But Jackson's partner, Con Sullivan, had enjoyed good luck in Idaho's Coeur d'Alene rush where he had staked a claim early on. He later sold out for $75,000, a tidy little sum at the beginning of the twentieth century. So the partners' spirits remained buoyant despite the hardships that lay ahead.

Regrettably, Con's good fortune did not follow him to Alaska when he chose Unimak over the Yukon and Klondike gold fields. Still, the four men landed on Unimak with a good grubstake and high expectations. They went ashore, unloaded their supplies, and set up camp near an old cabin. After a quick lunch they went back out in their rowboat to the *Lizzie Colby*, anchored out in the bay, to bring in the balance of their gear. The partners worked up a sweat pulling in to the beach and packing their supplies inland. They went back to the schooner for the night, planning to bring in the final load the next morning. After breakfast, the men got a late start and did not make it ashore until about noon.

As they closed on the beach, Rooney yelled out that he saw two men stealing their gear. This observation got their dander up. Without stopping to think things through, the four partners put their backs into the rowing, made landfall, and ran up the beach toward the creek bed where the thieves had made their escape. As they went through their camp they noticed that everything was gone. Rooney ran back to keep an eye on the rowboat while Florence ran to the cabin to check on things there. Con and Jackson checked out the trail along the creek bed quickly and then went down to the beach to see if there was a dory there that the thieves might use to make their escape. After about half an hour they met up again with Florence at the cabin and agreed that they would hike up the creek trail.

As they made their way along the creek the men split up to look for sign. Suddenly, shots rang out. They counted four, but saw no muzzle flashes or smoke. Then they saw him. Fred

Hardy, the triggerman, had been crouching behind a large rock when he fired the first rounds. He stood up to reposition himself for a better shot. The partners stood in shock, seemingly frozen in time by the stunning course of events. They must have wondered what had happened. Who was this rifleman trying to kill them over a few thousand dollars' worth of gold-mining equipment and camping gear? Then it suddenly became clear that Hardy's first volley had hit Florence. The man lay dying on the damp soil, quivering faintly. There was nothing anyone could do for him now. Then he was motionless.

Fred Hardy came from Lexington, Ohio, where he had been born in 1876, the same year that another Ohioan, Rutherford B. Hayes, was running on the Republican ticket for the office of President of the United States. The year he left Lexington for good, Hardy had worked as a telegraph operator, but in 1897 he went to Columbus and enlisted in the United States Cavalry. His timing was poor. Shortly thereafter, the U.S. declared war against Spain to free the Cubans from their colonial rulers. The U.S. Navy struck the first blow of the campaign in the Philippines. After dispatching the Spanish Navy in Manila Bay, the U.S. Navy landed soldiers on the islands. The U.S. Army worked closely with Filipino freedom fighters to defeat the Spanish colonial forces and remove them from the islands they had controlled for centuries. Hardy went ashore with this American expeditionary force in September 1898.

While the Spanish did not put up much of a fight and quickly gave up possession of the Philippines, the Filipinos demanded independence and set up their own democratic institutions and held elections. The U.S. got more than it bargained for in this campaign. It refused to recognize this nascent democracy. Instead, it sent in an occupation government. The ensuing guerrilla insurgency lasted for several more years. The U.S. finally destroyed this independence movement, but not before killing perhaps hundreds of thousands of Filipino freedom fighters and their civilian supporters. Nearly five thousand American soldiers lost their lives in the process.

It was a long, hard slog for the army during the brutal Philippine campaign. At some point during this dirty war, Hardy ran afoul of the army. Military police arrested him, and the army sent him back to the States to serve time at Alcatraz. During his incarceration there, Hardy spent so much time reading dime-store novels that the other inmates called him "Diamond Dick," after his favorite fictional character.

Upon his release from Alcatraz, Hardy headed to the Far North to seek fame and fortune, like so many other men at the turn of the twentieth century. He hired on to a fishing schooner called the *Arago*, jumping ship at Unimak and making his way inland. Within a matter of days he perpetrated his attack on the four prospectors. In the end, fortune eluded him, but he did achieve lasting fame, dubious though it may have been, as the first man legally hanged in the Territory of Alaska. It may surprise some to learn that the State of Alaska, the so-called Last Frontier, has never had the death penalty. During the Territorial days, though, a total of eight men were legally executed by the federal authorities, starting with Hardy in 1902. Two of these men were white, three were Native Alaskan, two were Black, and one, called Mailo Segura, was listed as "race unknown." More significantly, during this era, the Territory convicted numerous white men of murder and sentenced them to hang, only to later commute their sentences to life in prison. Many Territorial observers recognized the racial discrepancies in how Alaska meted out the death penalty. Largely due to this issue, the Territory eventually rescinded capital punishment in 1957, two years prior to statehood.

In addition to the men executed by Territorial authorities, several people were hanged under the so-called miners' laws. The 1884 Organic Act, which established Alaska's first laws and legal system, authorized a Territorial governor and created a Territorial court located in Sitka, along with one marshal, one attorney, and four court commissioners. This system was charged with covering a territory of roughly 600,000 square miles. That represents a land base two and a half times the size of Texas! Because the act also implemented the so-called Oregon Code, under which only taxpayers could serve on juries, it was not possible to legally try anyone in the Territory because there was no system to tax residents until 1899. In that year, the U.S. Congress addressed the problem with a new code to deal with criminal procedures in Alaska.

Although the Organic Act of 1884 left a few legal issues unresolved, it did provide for the extension of federal mining laws to the Territory. This allowed Territorial authorities to organize districts which elected local recording officers. These simple structures served for many years as virtually the only local governmental institutions in Alaska. They also provided the only mechanism to handle legal affairs in mining camps. When crimes were committed and alleged perpetrators captured, the miners of a given district came together to organize ad hoc miners' courts with three possible penalties for those found guilty of a crime. Those convicted of murder were hanged, those convicted of assault or theft were banished, and those convicted of all other offenses were fined according to the severity of the offense.

Such legal concerns did not enter Owen Jackson's mind on the day of Hardy's attack. Although it seemed impossible for him to believe, Florence was dead. Jackson and the other two men found themselves in a fight for their lives. They beat it down the creek bed as fast as they could go with the aim of making it to the boat, pushing out into the bay, and going to inform the authorities. Hardy and an alleged accomplice worked hard to prevent the implementation of this plan. The two murderous thieves initially planned only on making off with the expensive

A rowboat out in the waters off Unimak Island in the Aleutian Chain, c.a. 1904. *Mary Whalen Photograph Collection, 1975-84-559. Archives. Alaska and Polar Regions Collections. Rasmuson Library, University of Alaska, Fairbanks.*

gear of the prospectors. When they got caught in the act, however, they responded violently.

One wonders about the impact the Filipino campaign had on Hardy, and, perhaps, on his accomplice. At least one writer has described Hardy as "depraved." Wanton he may have been, but Hardy was not crazy. In fact, he was downright methodical, maybe even mechanical, as he pulled the trigger without hesitation. Had the army created a monster, or simply trained one?

As the retreating men neared the boat, Rooney, beading up with sweat and struggling to catch his breath, frantically yelled for the other two men to hurry up. "Poor Florence," he cried several times. Hardy's aim had been deadly. When Con Sullivan and Jackson made it to the rowboat, another shot rang out. A stunned Rooney reeled from the impact, fell to the sand, and let out a cry of shock and pain. Other shots followed rapidly. Hardy and his accomplice kept up a steady fire that peppered the boat and the beach and kicked up gravel and sand. It sent the fleeing men into a fog of panic. As they sought what cover they could behind the far side of the boat, Con assessed their desperate situation. Hardy and his accomplice were pursuing them with relentless intensity. There really was only one hope, and that was to make a break for it. Otherwise, they would all die right where they lay.

Jackson steeled himself and advised his friends to make haste. As he spoke, Hardy fired another round. The bullet instantly thudded into the boat, sending up a burst of splinters. At that moment all three rose in unison and moved toward the bluff. It was like a nightmare in which they seemed to move in slow motion. Their feet, clad in heavy rubber boots, felt mired in thick mud. Meanwhile, the two assassins pursuing them moved steadily and quickly to close the gap.

As the three men put about 15 or 20 yards between them and the rowboat, Hardy stopped to aim. Another shot rang out. Instantly Con screamed, "Oh Lord, oh Lord!" Hardy had fired a round that had slammed into his upper back between the shoulders. Con crumpled instantly onto the beach. With machine-like precision, another shot rang out; this one hit Jackson in the leg. The impact threw him down onto the sand hard. Jackson saw the blood begin to flow, and then looked back at Con lying in agony on the beach. Hardy and the other killer were relentless with their fire. Lead slammed into the rocks behind Jackson and whistled above his ears. He had no time to lose, so he moved toward the water, trying to find some cover. Then he saw Rooney moving around the point. Rooney signaled for him to join him. Somehow Jackson made it, and the two wounded men lay down on the ground next to each other. Hardy and his partner closed on them rapidly.

Rooney appeared to lose his nerve and will to fight for survival. "For God's sake," Jackson recalled screaming to Rooney, "pick up courage and let's try to get out of here." But Rooney remained frozen in place. "There's no use," he responded morosely. "We are all going to be killed." The two men could see one of their assailants going through Con's pockets. Jackson pleaded with Rooney one more time. Now was their only chance. They had to move while the killers focused on the contents of their dead friend's pockets. Rooney simply shook his head and remained frozen with fear on the beach.

Jackson, bleeding from his wounded leg, decided to make a break for it on his own. He jumped to his feet and ran for a bluff located a short distance down the beach. When he got there he climbed up a cliff and watched. Hardy had found what he was looking for in Con's pockets and got up to see what the other prospectors were doing. He only saw Rooney lying in the sand near the bluff. Hardy moved deliberately toward the stricken man. When he came up to him, Hardy immediately lifted his rifle to his shoulder and pulled the trigger without a thought. The bullet finished Rooney. Hardy then surveyed the shoreline, beach, and inland, looking for the fourth man. He saw nothing move. Satisfied with his work, the vicious killer signaled to his partner and they both headed inland without any effort to hide their lethal deeds.

Up on the bluff, Jackson stirred into action. As Hardy shot and killed Rooney, Jackson quickly slipped off his gum boots and took off. He ran all day and through the night, and did not stop until midnight the next day when he came upon a deserted cabin. In the morning, as he prepared to move again, he noticed two Natives approaching. Jackson bolted the door, fearing that they were part of the gang that had murdered his comrades. He waited for three more days in the cabin before he decided it was safe to move again. Then he headed out on the trail to make for False Pass, a Native village on the Isanotski Strait, an important shipping lane connecting the Gulf of Alaska to the Bering Sea. He finally stumbled into Scott's Camp, where prospectors eventually discovered him huddled under a dory, exhausted and nearly starved.

Jackson remained immobilized for two weeks. After he had regained his strength, the prospectors flagged down a steamship called the *Newport* and sent Jackson on to Dutch Harbor. The U.S. marshal from Nome, Frank Richards, greeted him there and took his statement. Officials then quickly dispatched authorities to Unimak Island to investigate the crime scene.

As far as Hardy was concerned, it had been a difficult but profitable day. He and his partner had not planned on shooting the prospectors, but had hoped instead to make off with their gear, unseen. Still, the affair had worked out to their advantage because Hardy stole more than $600 in cash from the dead men to go along with all of the gear. He seemed a little irritated that one man had escaped, but with that bleeding gunshot wound to the leg and no boat, Hardy was confident that the man would soon die in the bush. In fact, Hardy felt so optimistic about his luck that he did not pursue Jackson. He also decided to stay on the island. Maybe he thought that the island Natives would be blamed. He never told anyone what he was thinking.

On July 23, 1901, Hardy made a stop at a roadhouse on Unimak. It just so happened that a U.S. deputy marshal called O'Sullivan was staying at the same house that night. While he was in the restroom, O'Sullivan noticed Hardy stuffing a golden nugget and watch into a little leather pouch. The deputy asked Hardy how he had come by those items. Unsatisfied with the man's response and noticing his nervous demeanor, O'Sullivan arrested Hardy on suspicion of murder. The deputy also found a rifle and $681 in cash along with a few other items that were known to belong to the slain Sullivan brothers. Hardy claimed that after he had jumped off the *Arago*, he'd wandered into the interior of Unimak until he stumbled onto a cabin inhabited by Charley Rosenberg and two partners. The men had had a cache, according to Hardy, that included the articles found on him at the roadhouse. Hardy claimed the money came from his mustering-out pay, received when he was released from the army and after his captivity at Alcatraz. Hardy claimed that he took the other items in question when Rosenberg and the partners went out to prospect. It was not the best alibi, and O'Sullivan placed him in jail on Unalaska Island to await trial for murder and robbery.

The trial began on September 2, 1901, with Judge James Wickersham presiding. In five days the jury returned a verdict of guilty. No one else was charged or arrested for the murder of Rooney and the Sullivan brothers. Owen Jackson told the authorities that he knew for a fact the shots had come from two different locations. Investigators of the crime scene verified Jackson's statement and his testimony in trial. Nevertheless, only Hardy faced justice for the act. The *Nome News* speculated that Hardy might have killed his accomplice after the crime so that he might have all of the loot for himself. Deputies did arrest George Aston, who also had jumped ship from the *Arago*. Aston claimed that he did not know of Hardy until after the three prospectors were murdered. There was no evidence to connect him to the crimes, so the authorities released him.

Wickersham sentenced Hardy to hang on December 6, 1901.

Hardy appealed all the way to the U.S. Supreme Court. His attorney contended, among other things, that the court should have issued a continuance to allow Hardy to gather depositions or actual witnesses who could testify that he was still on board the *Arago* when the murders were committed. The writ of error only delayed the implementation of the verdict. The Supreme Court agreed with the ruling in the lower court, and Hardy was scheduled to hang on September 19, 1902.

Hardy was moved to Nome to await his fate. His jailers reported that Hardy remained cheerful and composed until the end. He continued to maintain his innocence, and even took up writing poems. More than a few jailers thought that Hardy began to lose his sanity. How else, they wondered, could one explain his strangely polite and pleasant demeanor during his incarceration on death row? Hardy maintained his innocence in the last statement he made before the noose was placed around his neck and the floor dropped from beneath his feet. Nevertheless, his protestations did not stop the Territory of Alaska from hanging its first convicted murderer.

Klutuk: "The Man from the Mountain"

The newspapers called him Klutuk, after the creek by which his cabin was located, up the Nushagak River near the Tikchik Lakes country. But he went by many different names. Eskimos called him "the giant" or the "man of the mountains." White trappers called him a "crazed Indian," the "mad trapper," the "wild man," or the "murderous monster." According to the *Cordova Daily Times*, Klutuk, a fur trapper of Yupik Eskimo heritage, killed as many as twenty people with an ax and a gun during a murderous career on the early-twentieth-century Alaskan frontier. His death has remained shrouded in ambiguity. Various people say he eventually died of natural causes, that he finally received frontier justice, or even that he would never die. Many Eskimos believe that he is a phantom lurking in the ice fog on the frozen upper Nushagak region of southwestern Alaska. There he skulks in the moon shadows of the scraggy black spruce, waiting to pounce on the unsuspecting who stray into the territory he so jealously guards against trespass.

Territorial authorities looked for Klutuk for years. Beginning in 1919, he haunted white and Native trapper alike in the region between Cook Inlet and the Kuskokwim River. In that year he reportedly killed two Natives and then boasted he would kill more people if he wanted. "It was no different than killing a moose," Klutuk was supposedly heard to say. Natives avoided speaking of him, and whites tried to downplay what they viewed as primitive superstitions. Nevertheless, fear of Klutuk spread far and wide throughout the isolated Kuskokwim country. It crept into the minds of even the heartiest frontiersmen like the icy breath of the north wind penetrating the chinking of a log cabin. Few people, Native or white, ventured into his rugged domain. In the summer, the vast and empty land patrolled by the phantom Klutuk was full of swampy muskeg and thick with mosquitoes. Natives utilized a few seasonal fish camps along the Kuskokwim and its tributaries. White fur trappers stayed away until freeze-up. Only after the ice formed on the rivers would they enter the region in the fall. They made arrangements for pilots to fly them out, or they packed out their cache of furs before spring breakup made traveling impossible.

By 1927, rumors of Klutuk's murderous deeds had spread widely through the camps and villages along the rivers and on the coast. Trappers reported sightings and told stories of feeling hunted like an animal while working their winter traplines. At five foot four and 140 pounds, Klutuk, a man in his mid-thirties during the height of his baneful reign, was not physically intimidating in the usual sense. But as the legend grew, so too did exaggerations of his cunning, wilderness prowess, and skill in the deadly sport of hunting man. He had, after all, dispatched Andrew Kallenvik near the little fishing village of Dillingham earlier that year. This murder was no small accomplishment, for Kallenvik was no tenderfoot, but a seasoned outdoorsman with a keen eye for trouble. He was also a large and powerful man, given to legendary bouts of bad temper and fits of violence when he drank. Once, in a drunken rage, Kallenvik broke into a home and severely beat a man and woman living there.

Kallenvik was camped with his trapper partner F. F. Peterson and their guide Butch Smith, waiting for the freeze-up of the Nushagak River that fall so they could head up to their winter traplines. The men planned to trap near Klutuk's lines that season, and Klutuk was not happy about their encroachment. He came into their camp with his famous black dog. Smith had heard the stories of a lone Eskimo trapper with a black dog who had recently killed trappers Charles Anderson and Arvid Sackarson for getting too close to his territory. He warily allowed Klutuk to remain in the camp, and when the opportunity arose, he warned his partners about the nature of their fireside guest. The three hatched a plan to send word to the authorities that Klutuk was in their camp. Smith and Peterson left the next day. They told Klutuk that they had to pack supplies over to the riverbank a few miles away. The sturdy Kallenvik stayed to keep an eye on Klutuk, but he started to drink to pass the time, and perhaps to calm his nerves. What exactly happened next is difficult to say, since Klutuk allegedly was the only surviving witness.

Somehow, he got the drop on the larger Kallenvik. Perhaps the burly trapper drank too much, and with his senses dulled and his guard down, Kallenvik allowed the cunning Klutuk to make his move. Regardless, when the partners returned to camp they found Kallenvik's lifeless body lying facedown in a coagulated pool of blood. A bloody ax that lay nearby, the large gash in the back of Kallenvik's skull, and the bullet hole in his arm told the story plainly enough. The two men needed no other details. They buried Kallenvik where he fell. Then they tracked Klutuk to a nearby slough, but there the trail turned into swamp. With few options, Smith and Peterson ended their pursuit and reported the incident to the Territorial authorities.

Tracking a man in a trackless wilderness is a thankless task. Just getting to the Kuskokwim Delta took Territorial deputy Frank Wiseman several months. He had to wait for freeze-up, for stormy seas to subside, and for a boat heading to Dillingham to pick him up. By then the trail was long cold. Finally, in January 1928, Wiseman heard rumors of a Klutuk sighting near Togiak. He caught a boat and trekked 50 hard winter miles by dogsled on what turned out to be a false trail. Territorial authorities were not pleased, but there was little the

Left to Right: Jack Dunn, Arnold Akers, Dolph Mespelt, Ed Whelan, Matt Bellon, Fred King. Taken At Medfra About 1934. All Upper Kuskokwim Trappers and Miners.

Men who hunted for pelts near Klutuk's haunts in the 1930s. *Fabian Carey Collection. 1975-0209-92. Archives. Alaska and Polar Regions Collections. Rasmuson Library, University of Alaska, Fairbanks.*

exhausted and exasperated Wiseman or anyone else could do at the time.

Gold panners and fur trappers provide Alaskan history with its most colorful and celebrated figures of the frontier era. The truth of the matter, however, is that capital investment and industrial exploitation fueled Alaskan development in the decades prior to World War II. Investment in large-scale mining was just beginning in the Kuskokwim region when Klutuk began his murderous reign. News spread by spooked trappers and Natives about the phantom of the frozen wastes threatened investor profits and slowed down the development of mineral resources in the region. Local lawmen groaned whenever rumors of Klutuk sightings materialized. Territorial officials, moved by the pressure of corporate interests, grew increasingly desperate to turn the phantom Klutuk into just another dead outlaw. The men who had to track Klutuk knew they would again be heading into a vast and empty land, chasing shadows and fighting bogs and mosquitoes or bone-chilling temperatures. No one relished the thought of hunting down the man from the mountain.

In the spring of 1928, however, Jack Aho was missing— another white trapper who had failed to show up to meet his friends at breakup. There were numerous things that could have gone wrong for Aho, but most everyone blamed Klutuk. Once again, duty called. Wiseman was soon back on the trail.

By June, Wiseman had little information to give to his superiors about the shadow he chased. He finally caught a cutter to Dillingham. On August 3, he made his way in two boats with a posse of six men. They went up the Nushagak River for 155 miles. The posse did not see a single human along the way until they made Koliganek, a small Native fish camp. At that location, Wiseman split up his party, sending one boat up the Tikchik River, while he continued up the Nushagak another 120 miles to the Chichitnok River. He went up this small tributary stream for another 30 miles. At that point, Wiseman called a halt to the pointless chase. All along their journey into the Interior they had investigated the cabins used by trappers and prospectors, including one Klutuk lived in. They found all of them abandoned, with no sign of recent human activity. In fact, with the exception of a few seasonal fish camps on the Nushagak, they saw no other sign that anyone had been in the region lately. With good reason, too; people stayed out of this boggy country in the summer months. The rivers offered the only means of travel and country subsistence, but they also teemed with grizzly bears. It was too rough to travel off the rivers and lakes, and darn scary to spend much time on the riverbanks in the brush.

After seventeen fruitless days of searching, Wiseman's posse returned to Dillingham to make a report. Territorial authorities and interested parties could do little other than accept the news that Klutuk remained on the loose and could be anywhere. Wiseman was a good lawman and tracker, and he had done his best. But how, he must have wondered, could one small search party hope to find a man who wanted to remain hidden in a trackless wilderness the size of the state of Oregon? No constituted authorities welcomed this manhunt; they all knew the hardships and the minimal expectations for success.

Nonetheless, Wiseman did not give up. Late the following winter, Wiseman found himself in the fishing village of Bethel, located at the mouth of the Kuskokwim River. There had been new sightings, mainly Eskimos reporting instances where community members said that someone had shot at them out in the bush. When something unexplained happened, increasingly, Eskimos blamed Klutuk. He began to take on a legendary status among villagers on the Kuskokwim River drainage. Klutuk was now big medicine in their worldview, a sorcerer with great powers to be respected, even feared. Although Klutuk stood no more than five foot four, the Natives began to speak of him as a giant. To this day, there are some who believe he is still alive and dangerous. He can control events and wield power over those who enter his territory.

Wiseman placed little stock in such talk. Moreover, the few credible reports that came in, Wiseman soon found out, turned out to be Native hunters mistaking villagers for animals they were hunting. Wiseman was willing to head upriver anyway to make a reconnaissance, but breakup had come early. Consequently, he found no one willing to guide him into the upper Kuskokwim wilderness at that time of the season. Wiseman returned to file another report about his failure to find the elusive Klutuk.

A federal official with the U.S. Geological Survey, B. D. Stewart, complained publicly that Klutuk's reign of terror was now negatively impacting the development of mining in the district. This complaint came at a crucial time in the Territory's history. The Great Depression had ravaged the Territory's fragile extractive economy. Officials wanted to exploit any opportunity for development—but the phantom Klutuk discouraged their efforts to develop the mining potential on the Kuskokwim.

More men were put on the case in the early summer of 1931. One of these men, a U.S. deputy marshal called Stanley

Nichols, ventured all the way up to the headwaters of the Mulchatna River, a small tributary of the Nushagak. In a cabin there he found the body of a man who, Nichols reported, had apparently died of natural causes. The newspaper report simply stated that Nichols identified the dead man as Klutuk. Officially, Klutuk was dead. Territorial authorities closed the Klutuk case; problem solved. Many old-timers, however, have raised questions over the years. Some believe that Klutuk's death was not natural; rather, it represented an example of frontier justice meted out by some individual or group of vigilantes. Others do not believe that the body found by Nichols was Klutuk.

Fred Hatfield was one of the nonbelievers. He told an alternate version of the demise of Klutuk based on an eyewitness account. His own, published in two different venues, created a minor literary controversy in the early 1990s. Back in the early 1930s, Hatfield had moved into the Kuskokwim region to run traplines in the winter and to fish out of Dillingham in the summer. He ended up spending some twenty years trapping in Alaska, and, over time, became an old-timer. One of the early pioneers that Hatfield befriended was Butch Smith, the man hired to guide Peterson and the unfortunate Kallenvik up the Nushagak in 1928. One day in 1934, Smith took the young Hatfield under his wing and began to ask about where he planned to set his traps during the coming winter. He told Hatfield that he knew of an exceptional region that was largely untapped by trappers far up the Nushagak in the Tikchik Lakes country. Smith, an occasional prospector in the region, had built a cabin several years earlier. It was far upriver in an isolated area that teemed with fur-bearing critters. Smith painted an alluring picture for the cocky young Hatfield. Like most greenhorns,

Hatfield desperately sought approval from hardened wilderness-savvy veterans. Smith appeared to be according him some respect for his frontier skills and strength. He was finally being recognized by the old-timers. He had made it; he was a heroic last frontiersman!

There was one catch, Old Butch warned: Klutuk. Not many true Alaskans were unaware of the tales of the old Eskimo phantom, but few had heard them from somebody who had direct knowledge. Smith told Hatfield about the death of Kallenvik. It would be dangerous to trap that far up the Nushagak, he warned, but then again, he must have thought the young Hatfield was ready for the challenge. Klutuk's cabin was a good 40 miles away from Smith's. The chances were good that Klutuk would never even know that Hatfield was there if he was smart and he played it safe. Hatfield boasted that he could handle Klutuk, phantom or man. That was the kind of talk that Smith expected to hear. While Hatfield was upriver, he could also check in on Smith's friend, Jake Savolly, who had failed to come downriver after breakup. The tenderfoot Hatfield took Old Butch's bait. He did not seem to realize his new confidant did not want to personally go up the Nushagak to look for his lost friend. Too dangerous up there with a crazy murderer on the loose! Smith had simply played on the young Hatfield's youthful pride.

Hatfield flew in to the upper Nushagak in the fall on Matt Flensburg's plane. He dutifully checked in at the cabin of Smith's friend Jake and found that it had been abandoned for some time. There was hardly anything there at all. Tired from his travels, Hatfield lay down on Jake's cot to get some rest. Not long after, he awoke to find himself covered in shrews nibbling at his clothes and skin. He jumped off the cot in horror, brushed the little critters off, and ran outside to calm down. As his head cleared from the sleep and the fright, he caught sight of something in the brush to the backside of the cabin. It was the remains of Butch's friend, Jake Savolly. Jake's bones had been picked clean by the shrews so that they looked, Hatfield later wrote, to have been polished. The way Jake's remains were placed, with arms outstretched, gave the appearance that his body had been dragged by someone to where it lay. That someone could only have been Klutuk, Hatfield quickly concluded. That explained why there was nothing useful left at the cabin. Klutuk had killed Jake and cleaned out his cabin. Hatfield knew that Jake represented Klutuk's fifth victim, and he wisely concluded that he did not want to be number six. He made up his mind right there to hunt Klutuk down and kill him.

Hatfield's self-serving story, told more than fifty years after the fact, had the makings of a John Wayne or Clint Eastwood movie script. He ratcheted up the bravado and inflated the lead character with an epic heroism grounded firmly on frontier common sense. He became, he wrote, a hunter of man. "If you know the habits of any animal, he's easy to trap," Hatfield boldly stated; "A man isn't [any] different." Hatfield's protagonist, the young Hatfield, just had to learn the habits of his prey. It was a simple, almost natural thing for a hunter to do. Study the prey and then trap it using the knowledge gleaned from observation.

Hatfield buried Jake and then went off to find Klutuk's trapline. In the first printed version of the story, he pulled up about thirteen traps, set them off, and threw them in the snow.

In the second, that number increased to twenty. He then circled all the way around Klutuk's trapline and doubled back in several places. Hatfield intended to throw Klutuk off, make him feel hunted, force him to stay put for the winter, or risk ambush anywhere at anytime. He believed that he had tied Klutuk up for the winter.

Hatfield traveled by snowshoe, a quiet and stealthier mode of travel than a noisy and unpredictable dogsled team, Klutuk's mode of travel. Hatfield surmised that Klutuk would not risk being discovered snooping around his cabin. Of course, that did not take into account the possibility that Klutuk, a man who lived off the land for extended periods, might have a pair of snowshoes somewhere!

When April came, Hatfield hopped on the plane owned by Matt Flensburg to head for Dillingham. He intentionally left behind everything except his fur pack. He was implementing a grand strategy—one that would take more than a year to accomplish. He expected Klutuk to see the plane, head for Hatfield's cabin, clean out the gear and supplies, and then lay in ambush for him upon his return the following season. Hatfield chuckled when he told his plan to Old Butch Smith in a Dillingham watering hole. Smith was upset to learn about the death of his friend Jake, and he seemed to be increasingly concerned for the safety of the cocky young greenhorn.

"Fred," Smith said, "Klutuk knows that you were there, and he is darn sure to be waiting for you to return since you left all your gear. What are you going to do?" Hatfield enjoyed hearing the frontiersman's concern. He told Smith not to worry, that he had thought everything through. He would not return to Smith's cabin, but would instead go to Harry's cabin on Rat

Creek, a little stream that connected Tikchik Lake to the river bearing the same name. Klutuk would see him fly in and know that he had been had. He would have to wait cautiously another year before he could lay another trap for Hatfield. But by this time, Hatfield would finally spring his own trap on Klutuk. Hatfield asked Smith if he could get his hands on some strychnine. Just a small dose of that would be enough to put down a grizzly bear.

Matt flew Hatfield in to Rat Creek and left him at the cabin with assurances that he would return in March. This would be early enough that Klutuk would have plenty of snow on the ground to get his dog team up to Rat Creek after he saw Hatfield fly out for the summer. Hatfield did not trap much that winter; he was too scared to get out much. When he did, he constantly looked over his shoulder. Being hunted frayed his nerves some. The cold, dark, and quiet of winter close to the Arctic Circle was tough enough to bear all alone. It became another thing altogether when you knew there was a phantom nearby waiting for the chance to kill you.

Hatfield passed a long and cold trapping season, staying close to his cabin in a constant state of alert. He even brought a Swede saw, a thin-bladed implement that made virtually no noise. While cutting wood he listened for dogs that would signal the presence of Klutuk. He lived with the feeling of constantly being watched. His mind played tricks on him. One evening Hatfield heard a strange tapping at the window of the cabin. He cautiously looked in the direction of the window so as not to give notice, but nothing was there. Then, there it was again. What was that tapping? Edgar Allen Poe would know. Was he beginning to hear things? He heard the noise again. He finally discovered a mink stabbed in the head deeply by two porcupine quills. Crisis averted, he took stock of the state of his nerves.

Seven months of this torture and it was finally March. It was time to set the trap for Klutuk. Matt would fly in soon to pick up Hatfield, so everything needed to be ready. Hatfield pulled out the leather bag containing his tins of tea and sugar—a staple item that could make any bad situation in the bush seem better. He knew that Klutuk would take them if left behind. That was his plan. He pulled out the strychnine package and carefully measured out two tablespoons of sugar to every quarter-size portion of the poison. Hatfield filled up his sugar tin in this manner, carefully packed everything away in the carry bag, and hung it from a nail on the log wall.

Not long after he readied the trap, Hatfield heard Matt's plane come in. He knew Klutuk heard it too, so he wasted no time gathering up the few items that he did not plan to leave behind. It would be darn good to see another human being after that long and lonely winter. He said hello to Matt and climbed aboard. Within hours they were back in Dillingham, and soon Hatfield was out in the bay on a fishing boat to earn a grubstake for next winter on the trapline. It was odd; Hatfield had been anxious to get back to Dillingham, but now found himself impatient to get back up to the Rat Creek cabin.

After an interminably long season of fishing, it was finally time to head back to the wilderness trapline. Hatfield flew back in with Matt, said his good-byes, and then cautiously headed to the cabin. He was not sure what to expect or what he might find. The tea and sugar, along with the traps, were gone, but everything else was just as he left it! Hatfield grew more confident—he began to think that he had won. He started to scout around the cabin looking for sign, and then started on down the trail Klutuk would have taken on his dogsled. Two miles away he found Klutuk's camp. Cautiously, he crept up close, until he saw that there were no dogs. More observation revealed that the camp had been mauled by grizzly bears. They had scattered gear everywhere and ripped the tent to shreds. Still no sign of Klutuk. Where was the phantom?

Finally, he saw what was left of a human skeleton covered in torn-up shreds of winter travel clothing. "My two years of feeling hunted," Hatfield wrote, "were over." He found Klutuk's .30-30 rifle, and removed the custom-made ivory sight. A trophy to be sure, but not for himself! He packed it away, buried the bones he had found, and left everything else behind. For the rest of the winter season he trapped where he pleased and went about his days and nights without a care. When he got back to Dillingham he proudly gave Old Butch the ivory sight. Klutuk was dead, he told the old-timer. He told no one else for fifty years, and trusted that Smith would remain true to the code of the frontier and say nothing to anyone.

Had justice been served? In the eyes of Territorial officials and the law, Klutuk had already been dead for several years before Hatfield made his first trip up the Nushagak River. When his story came out in the 1980s, it gained Hatfield quite a bit of notoriety back east, where he had gone to retire from his life on the Last Frontier. When old-timers in Alaska heard about it, they too became interested, but mainly because they did not believe Hatfield's tale. If he did poison someone, then it was an innocent man, some said. Hatfield should be arrested, they argued, because there is no statute of limitations in Alaska for murder. Others were infuriated with Hatfield because it was a commonly recognized right on the frozen Alaska frontier to make use of shelter and food when one got into trouble. Many speculated that the man Hatfield claimed to have poisoned was not Klutuk, but some poor, unsuspecting traveler who needed shelter and food. Nothing ultimately came of these debates, but the controversy surely helped sales of Hatfield's published memoir.

Who was Klutuk? Did he really kill a score of people? How did he die? No one can answer these questions today with any certainty, and we will probably never know. But the story of Klutuk reveals elements of a way of life that has long since disappeared, along with the values and beliefs held by people on that long-ago northern frontier.

Ed Krause

A heavy southeast gale battered a southeast Alaskan islet among the Sukoi on a cold and dark night in 1915. Calvin Barkdull, a fox farmer and the only inhabitant, didn't worry much. He hunkered down in his warm cabin with a confidence that comes with experience, a good supply of food and fuel, and a cozy bed. He planned to ride out the storm with style. Barkdull embraced his simple life. Many of his friends and family openly worried about his decision to live alone on an isolated island in Southeast Alaska's famed Inland Passage, but he was a twentieth-century fur trapper and entrepreneur. Ghost stories of pirates, renegade Indians, and murderers prowling about in the lonely Alexander Archipelago would not deter him.

There was a huge demand in Europe for rare blue fox pelts especially, and he hoped to cash in on it. They often fetched as much as $175 apiece. Multiply that by 100 to 150 pelts, and a good year might bring in about $20,000. Not a bad return on a capital investment of about $4,000 and several years of work in the early twentieth century. It was a pretty good deal for those who could handle the isolation and initial start-up costs. One needed a government permit, a small boat and some supplies, feed, and some breeding pairs to stock the islet. Pen the breeding stock, construct a crude shelter, and watch the proliferation of your "herd" of fox. If the international markets held, the weather cooperated, and the poachers failed to decimate the stock, a fox farmer was almost guaranteed good returns on his labor.

And, it turns out that the isolation of the fox farmer's life was somewhat exaggerated. In addition to the many fishermen who stopped in to chat, or the occasional marine emergency that brought refugees on unexpected visits, there were many unscrupulous types who took advantage of the minimal presence of constituted authorities in the Inland Passage. Barkdull had dodged bullets on a few occasions to defend his fox farm from outliers who sought to reap his harvest. He did work hard, but he had plenty of unwanted company to prevent him from feeling lonely.

On that stormy night, he was about to have more. At 10:00 p.m. he heard the islet's early warning system. Scores of foxes began to bark and wail in unison to produce what for the uninitiated would be an eerie noise. Barkdull feared the worst; it was probably a gang of poachers led by Ed Krause. He had been expecting them ever since his friend, a man called Callahan, had visited some time earlier. Krause, his guest told him, had boasted about constructing fox pens on his island. He intended to fill them with foxes that he would take from fox farmers on neighboring islands. Keep an eye out for that devil, Callahan had cautioned. Not long after he left Barkdull's operation, Callahan vanished without a trace. Then the Krause gang took over his fox farm. One day in town, a gang member who bumped into Barkdull audaciously told him of their plan to possess his furs at the end of the season. "So keep up the good work and have them ready for us," he had added with a hearty laugh.

Tragically, Callahan was one of many men who went missing in this part of Alaska between 1913 and 1915. Barkdull was determined not to be added to this growing list. He took stock of his perilous situation, and oddly, found himself annoyed that Krause had picked such a foul night to be on the prowl. With nearly two feet of snow on the ground, the mercury had dropped to about 0 degrees Fahrenheit, and that mean southeaster had created a wind chill of about 30 below. Well, that was life on the last frontier, and it would not do to cry about the situation. So Barkdull cleared his mind of sleep, assessed the situation, and then sprang into action. He realized that he held the advantage, thanks to the wake-up call from the foxes. Krause did not get the drop on him. And although it might be cold and miserable outside the cabin, he remained dry and warm. Tough duty for poachers tonight, he thought.

His confidence buoyed, Barkdull scrambled out of bed and dressed himself for battle in the dark. The last accessory that he adorned himself with was his loaded automatic rifle. He might be alone against a murderous gang of thieves, but that weapon was an equalizer. He silently congratulated himself on his decision to make that purchase. It had been a costly item, but Barkdull was a man who liked to be prepared for anything. That night he was ready to show the Krause gang some good old Alaskan hospitality if push came to shove. He figured he could serve up the lead in appropriate amounts to as many as a dozen or more unwanted visitors.

As he mused about how the lead would taste to his surprised and unwanted guests, Barkdull peeked out of the cabin's north window. Out in the little bay he just made out Krause's small boat coming around the north point to drop anchor. It had a distinct aft cabin with three oval-shaped windows. No doubt about it—the Krause gang was coming. Barkdull's watchdog, tied out near the boathouse, let out a racket when Krause came ashore in a rowboat. The poacher made for the cover afforded by a woodpile. There he crouched with a rifle to scan the scene and assess the situation.

Barkdull stayed put and kept watch. Then, suddenly, he heard a few shots coming from the other side of the small island. Outside by the woodpile, Krause strained a little to see if the gunshots would draw Barkdull out of his cabin to investigate. Instantly, Barkdull understood Krause's plan. He would have made an unsuspecting target had he not known that Krause was waiting in ambush. Calmly, he kept watch on Krause. The stove cranked out heat. He remained comfortable while the would-be thief and murderer shivered outside in the storm.

Krause no longer skulked behind the woodpile, but now actively moved about and stomped his feet in his losing bid to prevent frostbite. It seemed fitting that this adversary would suffer so much. With a wind chill approaching 30 below, Krause would not have the stomach for much more of this business. To emphasize the irony of the situation, Barkdull stoked up his fire. He kept an eye on Krause, whom he knew to be a crack shot. He did not want to give away his exact location, but he did want to pour on the heat . . . into his cabin, that is. He noted that Krause had shifted his position and he began to fear that the gang might try to smoke him out. He stoked up the fire to a blazing heat and sent black smoke pouring out of the chimney. This deliberate effort let the gang know that he was on to them and that he could pick them off if they came nearer to the cabin. The plan seemed to work. Barkdull watched the small boat go back out to the ship two times, and then saw the anchor go up and the small ship slip out of sight.

He knew the gang would return, so he quickly packed up his 125 blue fox furs, worth almost $22,000 in London, and

A fox farm on the beach of Kayak Island, Alaska, c.a. 1917. *Curtis R. Smith Photographs. 1997-59-26. Archives. Alaska and Polar Regions Collections. Rasmuson Library, University of Alaska, Fairbanks.*

caught a ride on a halibut boat the next morning. He was soon in Petersburg. There he shipped his package off through the Express Office operated by Wells Fargo. The season's work safely off to London, Barkdull eased on down the boardwalk through town with a feeling of relief.

When he saw Krause talking to a large group of men, Barkdull pushed his way through the crowd and gave him a piece of his mind that he would not soon forget.

"Krause," he said, "you're a cold-blooded, low-down sneak-thief, and a murdering skunk. There's a yellow streak up and down your back a foot wide. You won't come out in the open and fight in daylight, alone. You have to have a gang to help you in your dirty work and murdering of innocent, hardworking people at night. I could have killed you a half-dozen times last night, but I didn't want to. I want to see the time when the law will catch up with you and you are hanged by the neck until you're dead."

Krause had reeled around when Barkdull started shouting. He took in the entire insulting harangue. When Barkdull had finished chewing him out, he stared at the outlaw and waited for Krause to respond. So did the dumbstruck crowd of onlookers. Krause did not say a word. The truth stings sometimes. He simply walked away.

The world that Edward Krause operated in was fluid, free-wheeling, and geographically extensive. An amazing mix of peoples and cultures came together in Southeast Alaska at the beginning of the twentieth century. Diverse Native cultures, the Tlingit, Haida, Eyak, Tsimshian, and others, had been there for perhaps thousands of years. The Russian America company added to the cultural complexity by bringing Russian, Aleut, and Eskimo workers with them to operations based at what is now Sitka. After the sale of Russian America to the United States in 1867, American corporate fishing and mining interests moved into the Southeast. Along with this flow of capital came Chinese, Japanese, and Pacific Islanders to work in the canneries, and a wide mix of Americans and Europeans to work in the mines and service and shipping industries that sprang up. A handful of small towns and outposts emerged during this early period of development.

While most of the working people in this region never made much more than enough to get by on, the bustle of activity and mix of people created opportunities for entrepreneurs to profit. This population was seasonal and highly transient.

People came and went as they made and lost fortunes or sought opportunity elsewhere. Whenever rumors of a new strike or job opportunities spread through the saloon districts in Juneau, Petersburg, or Sitka, the populations of these towns could drop substantially. Newcomers were always coming in, though, and people who had made it big or lost everything seemed to make either celebrated departures or hasty retreats.

Resources for public safety were perpetually short in the Territory. This situation was unfortunate for law-abiding citizens, because this environment of shifting fortunes attracted con men, card sharks, thieves, and murderers. Ed Krause and his ilk were comfortable operating in the island world of Southeast Alaska. It was difficult to keep track of the mobile population. In addition, the extensive shipping traffic that linked the numerous islands and communities of Southeast Alaska's Inside Passage provided the unscrupulous with plenty of opportunities for foul play. Often, the absence of people who went missing was not noticed for weeks or months. Disposal of evidence, especially when the crime included murder, was facilitated by the vastness of the region's waters and the many uninhabited islands and bays. Ed Krause may have begun as one of the nameless throngs of adventurers and fortune seekers who made their way to Alaska, but he soon made a name for himself in Juneau as a Socialist Party activist, gang leader, and black marketer. He initially kept a relatively low profile, until a number of people went missing mysteriously after 1913.

It was not unusual for individuals to come and go, but it was strange when the people who disappeared left without settling their economic interests. It became less mysterious to the people of Juneau when Krause suddenly began to acquire the property and interests of those who'd gone missing. Suspicions cannot be acted upon legally without some evidence. Krause was developing a reputation for dastardliness, but nothing could be proved in the Territorial or city courts. Still, men of substance and property didn't just disappear. The good citizens of the Juneau area fraternal associations began to take action. When they hired a private investigator, Territorial officials began to pay attention. Vigilante justice would set back development a good many years. It was conceivable to the officials that the locals might even create a private security force. Regulator movements were a well-known aspect of numerous Wild West communities. It would be difficult to stop the violence once it began, and to separate the law-abiding from the outlaws. Lines between right and wrong often blurred when constituted authority broke down and the citizenry took matters into their own hands. Something would have to be done.

Krause became the prime suspect in several of the disappearances. Among the missing was Captain James Plunkett. He owned a charter vessel called the *Lue*. Plunkett occasionally stayed in his cabin near Juneau, but mainly spent his days and nights on his boat, taking people anywhere they needed to go. As a matter of course, Plunkett was gone often, but the manner in which he disappeared had many people talking. It just plain didn't make sense. On October 24, 1915, Plunkett, while in a cigar shop on Front Street, received a request for a charter to Snettisham. He had to turn the man down because he had already committed to take a passenger to an undisclosed location. When the *Lue* left the Juneau docks a few days later, nobody thought there was anything unusual about it. It was, however, the last time that anyone in Juneau ever saw

Plunkett again. What was strange about this case was that the United States Customs Office in Juneau reported that it had received a letter signed "Plunkett" that reported the *Lue* had been destroyed by fire. The envelope contained Plunkett's boat license. An investigation would later reveal that Krause had typed the letter on his typewriter and had signed Plunkett's name. Although searchers never found Plunkett's body, the Territory eventually charged Krause with murder.

Krause was also suspected in the disappearance of a Japanese foreman at a mining operation near Petersburg. Kato Yamamoto owned real estate in the British Columbia area. The bank in British Columbia demanded a foreclosure, since it was conjectured that Yamamoto had drowned. Nobody believed the story. It did not make sense to anyone who knew the hard-working Japanese man. He was educated, had money; in fact, he was owed hundreds of dollars in wages by the Olympic mine. There was no good reason for him to simply walk away from his life. But then, there was no reason for any of the other men, including Olaf Ekram, O. E. Moe, and William Christie, to go missing.

The Christie case was especially troublesome. He had recently married a pretty young German girl called Cecile. As the authorities investigated his case, they discovered that Krause had had a relationship with Cecile not long before Christie began to see her. Krause was not happy when Cecile broke off their relationship, and became jealous when he learned of her new beau. He did not, however, let on in public that he was upset. The hearsay evidence suggested that he kept his jealousy to himself while he plotted revenge against Christie, and reconciliation with Cecile. On October 29, 1915, Krause's brazen behavior reached a new level. In broad daylight he abducted Christie by posing as a deputy marshal. He presented a forged warrant for the arrest of his young rival to the foreman at the Treadwell Mine where Christie worked. The ruse worked; Krause falsely arrested Christie and told him he had to take him to Juneau. Krause marched Christie down to the dock and onto his boat. Barkdull's friend, Charlie Kinney, was in his boat near the dock and saw the two get on Krause's boat. He was the last man, besides Krause, to see Christie alive.

Back in town, Cecile wondered what had happened to her husband. Clues began to emerge. Soon, Cecile received a note purportedly from Christie explaining his absence. Interestingly enough, Krause was spotted near the Christie home about the same time that the note arrived. Christie had been a Mason, and the local lodge assisted Cecile in her efforts to find her husband. It publicized a reward for any information about his whereabouts. Kinney heard about the reward and told them what he had seen. Krause was now the prime suspect.

With the pressure increasing, Krause realized that officials were closing in on him. Witnesses reported seeing him on a boat to Ketchikan. In Ketchikan he booked passage on a passenger ship, the *Jefferson*, under an assumed name, O. E. Moe, a missing person at that time from Juneau. The law finally had caught on to Krause, and the authorities in Seattle were alerted to his flight. Somehow, Krause managed to disguise himself and walked right past the officer waiting for him at the gangplank. But for the efforts of a former Alaskan who was now a salesman in Seattle, Krause might have made good his escape. As Krause walked down a Seattle street, the citizen pointed him out to the police. They arrested him immediately.

Krause tried to pass himself off as Moe, but it became clear that the police weren't buying it. Krause began to come clean and put his energy into fighting extradition. He lost that battle, and was soon back in Juneau facing trial for a litany of major crimes, including kidnapping and murder. The jury found him guilty of kidnapping Christie and murdering Plunkett, even though there was only circumstantial evidence in the latter case. Krause's reputation was such in Juneau that the jury had heard enough and wanted to prevent him from harming anyone else ever again. He was sentenced on May 11, 1917, to be hanged.

Krause had other plans, though. His gang in Petersburg had been working out a plan to liberate their boss. Somehow, Barkdull heard rumors of what they intended to do. He wrote a letter to the Juneau court warning that Krause's gang planned to get into trouble so that at least one of them would be thrown in jail, giving him the chance to smuggle in a hacksaw. The court thanked Barkdull for the information, but evidently put no stock in the warning. Within days, a drunken member of Krause's gang threw a beer bottle through a window in a Juneau bar. He was arrested and thrown in jail. That same night Krause put the smuggled saw to good use, cutting through the bars of his cell. He headed down to the docks, hopped into a rowboat, and made for Admiralty Island.

Pete Early, James Mahoney, and James Estes were the night guards on duty at the Juneau jail. Everything was in order when their shift began at 4:00 p.m. When 9:00 p.m. rolled around, they routinely prepared for the night shift. Men had to be put in their cells and the fires stoked. Early went to the back of the jail to take care of the fires while Mahoney and Estes went down the long corridor that separated the cells from a large block. As

Estes called out "All in," a voice came back saying to hold for a minute. Something was not right. A few seconds later Mahoney and Estes heard the slam of a door that separated the big holding tank from the rest of the jail cells. It was a door that the two guards had just passed through moments earlier. Mahoney reacted instinctively and ran toward the door; having found it closed, he tried to open it. A wooden peg had been placed in the clasp to lock them in the large tank. About that time, the guards realized that Krause was missing from his cell, and one ran outside to fire two warning shots. The noise raised a general alarm in the town. Men in Juneau heard the alarm shots and began to make their way to the jail. Within minutes a throng of men waited to hear what the plan would be to track the "murderous monster" down. After a quick informal meeting in the attorney general's office, official instructions were delivered to the men gathered outside. Search parties, armed with weapons from the jail armory, were sent in every direction.

The governor had ten men put into a car to drive down the Salmon Creek road, while other men went on foot to scour the town and trails. Juneau is a small waterfront town located on a narrow channel. It sits on a thin flat and is backed up against steep glaciated mountains that appear to rise up out of the Inland Passage. These steep mountains are nearly impassable on foot. With only a few roads and trails, Krause would be easy to find if he remained on land. With that knowledge, several launches were sent out to the main Inland Passage communities of Petersburg, Sitka, Point Retreat, and to the other side of Douglas Island. Communication efforts were made to notify as many vessels as possible to be on the lookout for the fugitive. There was a growing conviction that Krause must have headed out for the open seas. He was simply too well known a figure in the Passage waters.

The conventional wisdom was wrong. In fact, Krause headed to Admiralty Island. News about the Krause escape traveled far and wide. People reacted in a variety of ways. Many single men excitedly joined the hunt, but family men reacted differently to the news that a desperate killer was on the loose. Arvid Franzen, about thirty-five years old and the father of six children, lived on the coast of Admiralty Island. When he heard the news, he grabbed a ride on the first boat home to protect his family at Doty's Cove. He had only been home for a short while when he caught sight of a small boat coming in toward the beach near his house. Incredibly, he sent his wife out onto the porch to clean as a diversion. Franzen told her to greet the stranger when he came up to the house! He assured his frightened wife that he would be right there behind her with a rifle trained on the man. Ask the man his name, he told her. If he says "Krause," it will be the last word he ever utters, Franzen guaranteed her.

Well, as one can imagine, the plan hardly calmed her nerves. Nevertheless, she did as he instructed. Krause landed, got out of his boat, and walked up the beach several hundred feet. With his hat pulled down over his eyes, he moved in a crouching gait toward Mrs. Franzen on the porch. About mid-way, he stopped, reached down, and grabbed a piece of steel about two feet long and one inch in diameter. If he looked a little hangdog before, his demeanor now seemed menacing. According to Barkdull's telling of the story, Krause coldly told the woman to get him something to eat. When she hesitated, he snapped at her that his name was Krause, and that he was used to having his demands obeyed. When the woman froze, he decided to give her a little motivation to obey his command. As he got close he lifted the steel into the air in an aggressive manner. A split second later, he lay dead on the boards of the Franzens' front porch.

A .25-35 bullet had fairly ripped through his body next to his heart and another had gone through his brain. He twisted and fell hard onto the porch. Sticking out of his clothing was a large case knife which had been turned into a hacksaw of sorts; this was the tool Krause had used to escape from the Juneau jail.

Franzen sent a letter off to Marshal Tanner through two Indians. It bluntly stated that he had just killed Krause and that he would like the authorities to remove the body. It unsettled his family to have it lying on the porch, he added. After showing the letter to the marshal, the Indian messengers took the letter to the governor at his mansion. At an inquest held a few days later, officials exonerated Franzen of any wrongdoing.

Franzen received a $1,000 reward that had been placed on Krause's head, dead or alive. The governor paid it to him out of the Territory's emergency fund. Krause had been convicted and sentenced to hang. His escape from the federal jail only changed the terms of his death sentence and prolonged his life for a few days. Franzen's wife was happy to have the entire ordeal over. Maybe things would now quiet down and get back to normal on their little beach at Doty's Cove. Then again, her husband had just killed one of the most notorious outlaws in Territorial history on her front porch. How does one get over that kind of excitement? Also, there was concern that one of Krause's gang might try to even the score. Franzen decided to carry a gun just in case. He received a special handgun permit from the United States Attorney in Juneau. The Krause gang seemed to disappear, however, and Franzen never had to defend himself against them.

Investigators found incriminating evidence in Krause's belongings. There was the mortgage worth $2,500 that had belonged to Yamamoto. Krause's typewriter contained carbon copies of letters he had written to officials detailing the loss of Plunkett's ship. But the outlaw took with him far more secrets than the evidence had revealed. Just what the extent of his murderous and plundering career was, no one could tell, save perhaps the bad man's lawyer, a man called Kazis Krauczunas. The Juneau *Daily Dispatch* reporter asked Krauczunas to tell what he knew about the extent of Krause's crimes. Perhaps the friends and relatives of his many victims could take some solace when the truth began to come out. Krauczunas responded in a letter to the paper, saying now that Krause was dead, it was best that everybody forget about him.

It is now nearly 100 years later, and people still have not forgotten about Ed Krause.

William "Slim" Birch

It was a loud and raucous night at the Douglas City Hotel in 1896. The ten-cent beer flowed as easily as the conversation between the miners and the good-time girls working that evening. William Birch, called "Slim" by those who knew him, made his way to the bar to slake his thirst. The smoke in the room settled over the large crowd of revelers like fog on a cold Juneau morning. Slim muscled through the crowd in front of the well and bumped into Henry Osborne, another local miner. Osborne shrugged it off as an unintentional gesture that went with the territory for those bellied up at the hotel bar on a busy winter evening. Osborne waited for the overworked bartender to bring the pint he'd ordered earlier; Slim called for one too. As the bartender finally made his way back to where Slim stood and Osborne sat, the two men waited with anticipation. The barkeep unintentionally set the pint down in sort of a no-man's-land between the two men. It was an ambiguous situation. Both men, anxious for a beer, reached for the glass. And that's when the trouble began.

Neither man conceded the glass of beer. They first exchanged insults and swore oaths. The tension built as the two men raised their voices and took the measure of their adversary. Suddenly, Osborne stood up from his stool, took a swing, and the scuffle began. Bystanders felt the concussion of their blows and tried to escape the sudden explosion of testosterone and violence as the two men fought it out in the crowded bar. The patrons enjoyed the spectacle, tried to stay out of the fray, and put money on one contender or the other. Such affairs generally run out of gas quickly unless scripted by Hollywood. This exchange did not last long. Neither man was in any shape for an extended brawl. As they ran out of breath their blows slowed and landed more softly. Finally, Osborne seemed to get the upper hand when he landed several clean hits to Slim's jaw that left the thirsty man stunned and on his knees. The whole affair lasted less than a few minutes. By that time, the proprietor of the establishment had restored order, preserved his investment, and encouraged the customers to satisfy their reinvigorated thirst.

As the fight concluded, energy pervaded the room. The spectators slapped each other on the back, laughed, cheered, and repeatedly recounted the exhibition they had just witnessed.

A group of men passing the time in a Douglas, Alaska, saloon at the beginning of the twentieth century. *Alaska State Library, Case and Draper. Photographs, 1898-1920, P39-0802.*

Osborne, feeling proud of his part in the affair, swaggered over to the bar to accept the accolades that go to the victor in such proceedings. He smiled as he rubbed his jaw a little, stood up tall, and drank the beer that had precipitated the fight. Then he headed out the door at the request of the owner. He went straight to the Standard Saloon to drink off the increasingly painful aftereffects of his battle.

Slim was a little slower to get up and move out of the Douglas City Hotel. After he had gone to the floor, his brothers Joseph and Robert, also in the bar that night, had set down their drinks and pushed their way through the crowd to come to his aid. Slim initially refused their assistance, but he soon allowed them to help him get up and shake off the effects of the roundhouse right to his jaw. After Slim had caught his breath and downed a drink, the three brothers made their way out into the damp Douglas night.

Douglas Island—in the Territory of Alaska—sat just across the Gastineau Channel from Juneau and the mainland. It traces its origins to the Treadwell mine, opened in 1881 by John Treadwell. The mine flourished until 1922, and was the largest gold mine in Southeast Alaska. It was a large-scale capital operation at four sites; one shaft went about 2,400 feet deep. Over the decades that it operated, it employed thousands of workers. It was significant historically as the first major privately capitalized mining operation in the Territory. It captured the attention of the federal government and forced Congress to pass legislation to create local laws and a Territorial governing structure. The Juneau-Douglas area became a boomtown, the first American community of any size and stature in the Territory. As such, it attracted a range of characters, some law-abiding and others not. By the late 1890s, the permanent town citizens proudly emphasized the community's orderliness and possibilities for investment. They did not stand for Slim Birch and his ilk. Slim soon found out that anything did not go in Juneau and Douglas.

Slim was still fuming as he and his brothers also made their way to the Standard Saloon to enjoy a few more rounds. It did not take long for the brothers to see Osborne drinking at another table. Later that evening, Slim made a move to obtain payback. This time when he squared off with Osborne, Joseph and Robert joined in. Although Osborne put up a good defense, the Birch brothers soon overwhelmed him. The men of the Douglas mining community were no strangers to fighting and other rough behavior. But miners nevertheless adhered to a code of frontier manhood that saw honor in defending oneself, so long as the fight was fair. To their disgust, Slim crossed over another line of frontier protocol that night when he bit off Osborne's nose and part of one of his ears. At that moment, the appalled onlookers rushed into the melee to Osborne's aid and to subdue the Birch brothers. When the authorities arrived, they got medical attention for Osborne and then arrested the three cowardly brutes and charged them with mayhem.

The Birch brothers went to trial shortly after their arrest. Joseph was acquitted of the charge. The jury found Robert guilty, and the judge sentenced him to a ten-month jail term and a $350 fine. On the question of Slim, the jury could not reach a decision. The Territory declared a mistrial and then retried his case. In the subsequent court case, a jury found him guilty. Slim received a sentence of three years' hard time at San Quentin.

Slim had bragged in court and at the jail that he would not go willingly to San Quentin. He made good on his word when he escaped from the Juneau jail on January 9, 1897, before he could be transferred to San Quentin. Masked men walked into the jail, attacked the lone guard, and sprung Slim from his cell. Slim quickly left town with his small gang and made for nearby Admiralty Island, a few hours by steamboat to the west. His coconspirators had planned well by preparing a cabin on the island located about 2 miles from the beach on Bear Creek. They stocked it with food and supplies, including numerous boxes of .38-90 and .45-70 cartridges, in case things got hairy. In addition, they modified the cabin by cutting out portholes in the log chinking up high near the roof, so that the overhang provided cover.

Slim was right to expect trouble. Officers and deputies from Juneau began the manhunt as soon as they found the bound and gagged jailer, a man named William Lindquist. Authorities inquired around town and down at the docks and kept the dragnet up. The marshal learned that four men had left on a boat in the middle of the night. Soon the manhunt extended to the outlying islands. Word soon spread as officials widened their search. They finally got a lead that the fugitives had made their way to Admiralty Island and now occupied an old prospector's cabin. Preparations began straightaway to charter a steamer called *Lucy*. Marshal William Hale led a posse comprised of Deputy William Watt, A. A. Bays, William Lindquist, and Sam Johnson, an Indian policeman. They steamed all day and night and arrived on the island on a Sunday morning. The posse immediately headed up Bear Creek Trail, confident that they would soon

surprise the outlaws and take them into custody with little or
no trouble.

When they saw the cabin, Hale, Watt, and Bays strode up
to the door, leaving Lindquist and Johnson back down the
trail to provide cover if necessary. Then one of the three men
knocked on the door. Instantly all hell broke loose. Inside, Slim,
Hiram Schell (a man who had served time in the Juneau jail
for robbing the Treadwell Mining Company), and two other
accomplices had heard the approach of the lawmen. Silently
they made their preparations. As soon as they heard the knock
at the door, they unleashed a volley of bullets through it. Outside, a hail of bullets and wood splinters engulfed Hale, Watt,
and Bays. As the officers recoiled in terror, the fugitives pushed
the door open and fired another salvo point blank at the retreating lawmen. The strategy proved effective. One of the shots
struck Bays in the thigh, opening up a nasty flesh wound. The
three lawmen fled from the cabin for the shelter of the tree line
nearby. Back in the cabin, one of the outlaws slammed the door
shut before he joined his partners in firing round after round
through the portholes they had cut earlier in the log chinking.

Under this storm of lead, the posse slowly worked its
way back away from the cabin in search of better cover. The
wounded Bays dodged from tree to tree as he tried to get out
of the line of fire. While the posse retreated, Slim and Schell
slipped out the cabin window in the back and headed up a
ridgeline above the cabin, where they could reposition themselves, unseen. They made their way to the hillside above the
cabin and then spread out to assume different points of fire.
Slim took a position about 80 yards to the right of the cabin on a
low hill in the tree line. From this position he taunted the posse

members, yelling, "You will try to catch Slim Birch, will you?" Then he opened up a deadly fire. The fugitives had caught three of the five members of the posse in a wicked crossfire.

During his retreat, Watt took a bullet in the leg that broke the bone in two places. He slowly worked his way to cover behind the exposed roots of a deadfall. A blood trail in the snow revealed the path he had taken. Bays, bleeding from the thigh, followed the gory trail and joined Watt. All the while, Johnson kept up a covering fire from the distant tree line that slowed down the rate of fire coming from the cabin and the ridge. This cover allowed the two wounded men to help each other withdraw as best they could, but they both knew they were in a tight spot. The rotten tree afforded little protection from the lead flying all around them. They tried to stop their bleeding, and then agreed that Bays would make his way down the Bear Creek Trail to the *Lucy* to get help.

Marshal Hale had been working his way from tree to tree, pausing to return fire when he could, and then seeking better cover. After Bays made for the beach, he tried to give Watt some assistance. Caught in the crossfire, he stayed to help his fallen comrade. The badly wounded Watt needed help. As Hale knelt by him to look at the leg wound, bullets whined above his ears and kicked up the snow and ice around him. Almost immediately, one of the pieces of flying lead fired from the cabin found Hale. It entered his left side in the back, just above his hip. Meanwhile, Lindquist had hidden behind a large tree about thirty paces in front of the cabin while bullets peppered the bark. He finally made a run for it. He heard Hale scream in pain when he got hit. Lindquist looked in Hale's direction and saw him drop near a small waterfall by the downed tree that insufficiently sheltered Watt. As Hale tried to move, he fell down over this waterfall and into the water. Watt tried to drag himself around the creek in the same direction, but it was to no avail; he was nearly used up.

Hale managed to get out of the crossfire a safe distance, where he met up with Johnson, who came to his aid. The two moved down the trail toward the beach. Somehow, Lindquist managed to scamper unscathed through the wall of lead flying around him. He too made his way to the beach. They reluctantly left their friend, who lay mortally wounded near the cabin. About a half-mile from the beach, Johnson and Hale stopped at a prospector's cabin to get some aid for the latter's wound. J. F. McWilliams, one of the two men who lived there, must have known about the Birch gang up the trail. They were desperate men, and he was none too happy to have them in his neighborhood. He had heard the gunfire in the distance, and so it came as little surprise to see the wounded marshal on his doorstep. But McWilliams lived a fair piece from the nearest law enforcement office. To aid the marshal invited retribution from Slim. The fearful McWilliams refused their request for assistance and sent them on their way.

When the posse retreated, the two fugitives firing from the cabin quickly gathered up a few supplies and headed out toward the south. Meanwhile, Slim and Schell stayed up on the ridgeline and made their way for about a mile in the same southerly direction until the trail merged with the one that their companions had taken. The four of them continued south toward Green's Bay, where they hoped to secure boat passage from Admiralty Island.

When Captain Yorke heard the echoes of gunfire back at the *Lucy,* he began to make his way up Bear Creek to offer assistance. He had not gotten very far when he met the wounded Bays limping down the trail. He helped Bays get on board the boat and then turned back up the trail, where he soon ran into Lindquist. Then he found Johnson helping Hale down the trail. The posse quickly related what had happened. Giving Watt up for dead, Yorke took the steamer to Juneau as fast as it could go. As they docked, the captain let loose with the steam whistle. Residents of Juneau heard the alarm and many came to the dock to learn what had transpired in the manhunt.

After hearing news of the shootout on Bear Creek, the authorities organized another posse of nineteen dependable men under the leadership of Captain William Martin. Determined to capture the small band of outlaws, the new posse quickly headed out on the *Rustler* to Admiralty Island. About four hours later, the captain ordered the ship to half speed when they neared the mouth of Bear Creek. In total darkness, Captain Martin ordered his men to load their weapons. Silently, the men placed cartridges into their Winchesters one round at a time. The posse expected more trouble. The only noise to be heard was the menacing click made for each round loaded as the men prepared to do their duty.

Carefully and noiselessly, the company landed on the snow-covered beach. They made their way up the dark trail until they came upon McWilliams's cabin. Captain Martin suspected that the two prospectors were in cahoots with the Birch gang. He told his men to surround the cabin, and then he gave the order to break down the door. Inside, the two miners jumped from bed in fright as the posse barged into their cabin with Winchesters leveled at them. Martin interrogated the wide-eyed men until he felt confident that they were not in any way connected to Slim. Still, McWilliams had refused to give aid and comfort to a badly wounded marshal. Martin told McWilliams to dress and then commanded him to lead the posse up to Slim's cabin so that they could recover Watt's body. McWilliams felt a bit more compliant on this night. He led the posse single file up the trail through a sparse growth of stunted trees and shrubs. In the nearly four feet of snow, this trek took some time in the lamplight. At about four in the morning they saw Slim's hideout about a hundred feet off in the distance. The group halted to look for Watt and signs of occupants in the cabin.

Martin called out several times but heard no response. He ordered three shots fired into the cabin. Again, the posse heard no response. Next, the captain ordered the men to attack the cabin in all haste. The company quickly rushed on the cabin, broke down the door, and streamed inside with rifles at the ready. They found the cabin empty and then paused to catch their breath and wait for the adrenaline rush to pass. The captain asked the men to spread out to look for Deputy Marshal Watt. They found his body quickly, about 150 yards from the cabin. Watt was faceup in the snow with his right fist clenched on his torso. Before he died he had managed to stick his rifle muzzle first into the snow, perhaps as a marker to help searchers find him. From the look frozen on his face, it was clear that the brave officer's last moments had been suffered in extreme pain. He had been shot twice, once in the leg, and once in the left side. The latter bullet had traveled upward and into his chest and likely caused his death.

The sight of Watt's body brought a silent melancholy to the company of men. They wrapped him up carefully and put him by the cabin and then they all crowded inside. After they lit a fire they searched for evidence and clues. Then they warmed themselves and tried to catch a few hours of sleep before daylight.

In the morning, Captain Martin's posse returned to the *Rustler* with Watt's body. Martin believed that the outlaws were heading for Green's Bay to catch a launch. Martin meant to get there first with his volunteers, but an insufficient coal supply on board forced them to steam back to Juneau to resupply. Within a matter of hours they had made the trip to Juneau and were heading back to Admiralty Island. First, they unloaded twenty men at Bear Creek to track Birch from his cabin overland to Green's Bay. The rest of the posse then steamed toward Green's Bay to meet them.

Slim and Schell had been traveling hard and fast. Slim knew that their bullets had hit more than one of the posse members. That would mean big trouble if they could not make a clean getaway. They moved so fast away from the cabin that they did not bring enough food. That is likely why the four men split into two groups. Slim and Schell continued on to Green's Bay. No one knows the identity of the other two outlaws or what happened to them. Slim and Schell made good time; the two kept moving in part to stay warm. They were not dressed appropriately for the elements. The only food they ate was a piece of venison that they took from an Indian. They told the man that they would kill him if he did not cooperate with them. Slim demanded that he paddle them across the bay. As they got into the Indian's canoe, they caught sight of the steamer, the *Rustler*. The fugitives changed their minds instantly and headed for the woods without saying anything to their Indian captive.

The overland posse arrived at Green's Bay about a day or so behind Slim and Schell. They found the *Rustler* waiting for them to show up. They had seen nothing of Birch or his gang along the trail. They asked around the small village for information and learned from an Indian that Slim and Schell had been nearby. The company spent the night in the boat, and in the morning they surrounded the small cluster of cabins at Green's Bay. They searched each one, but Slim and his partner had snuck away into the woods. A search party set out immediately, and by 9:00 a.m., an Indian had discovered the two men lying under a blanket in between two fallen trees. Within a matter of minutes Captain Martin and the posse surrounded the two men. Two members leaped onto the blanket shielding the sleeping outlaws. The two fugitives offered almost no resistance. Slim feebly attempted to draw a revolver, but it was quickly taken from him. Their flight from the cabin and subsequent days of exposure to the cold with little food to eat had taken a physical toll on them.

Exhausted from their time on the run, they sat there in stunned silence. Finally, with a little reservation in his voice, Slim looked at one of the men in the posse and said, "Hello, Pete—I'm glad to see somebody here I know." Pete said little as members of the posse bound Slim and Schell with cords. The prisoners were taken on board the *Rustler* and put under watch until another steamer, the *Seaolin*, arrived to take them, bound in iron manacles, to Sitka, to await another trial.

At trial, Slim's lawyer made a case for self-defense in the death of Watt and the wounding of Hale and Bays. For his part,

Schell claimed that Slim had threatened to kill him if he did not play his part in the gunfight at Bear Creek. The Territorial attorney was hamstrung in building his case because he could not find any witnesses; all of the key witnesses had moved on to new diggings. Slim and Schell were acquitted of murder charges, but Slim still owed the Territory three years at San Quentin on his mayhem charge.

Nellie "Black Bear" Bates and William Schermeyer

It was May 1923 in Iditarod, Alaska, the time of breakup when the snow melts and the ice goes out of the rivers. It is a time of great promise and relief for the people of the Far North. Alaskans don't get too excited about spring. The famous Johnny Horton song reveals the reason for this northern indifference to the third week of March. The chorus says it all: "When it's springtime in Alaska, it's forty below." Breakup, usually in May, is the important sign of warmth that the sourdoughs wait for. After eight months of winter, the warmth of the sun returns and the trees and plants once again turn green.

For Nellie "Black Bear" Bates and her partner in crime, Bill Schermeyer, it was an especially memorable breakup season. The two stood in the empty parlor of his locked and boarded-up Iditarod Roadhouse. Schermeyer smiled nervously as he alternately peered out the window and then glanced at Black Bear. At first glance one might have thought that the leaves were popping from their buds right there in front of the two criminals, inside the roadhouse. A more thorough examination, however, would have revealed the true explanation for the apparent indoor foliage.

Black Bear was furiously working with a hot iron with an intensity one does not usually bring to such a chore. Schermeyer knew that he should stay focused on his watch, but he could not help himself; he just had to watch Black Bear. Who could resist such a view? Here was one of the most famous prostitutes of the Far Northern mining frontier standing in his roadhouse at the ironing table. There was a damp canvas sack on the floor by her side. Black Bear kept reaching down to put her hand in the sack in an intense effort to dry thousands of dollars in damp currency. The bills were hanging on the furniture and shelves and some had fallen like leaves on the floor around Black Bear. Yes, it was hard for Schermeyer to remain focused on his watch. The spring-like view inside captivated him in a way that springtime in Alaska never had.

The canvas sack had contained $30,000 in cash and had been buried in the snow some distance from the roadhouse for much of the winter. Now, with the bills dried, it was time to divide the loot, find safer and longer-term hiding places, and wait until things cooled down and it was safe to begin to use the money. Black Bear chose to use mason jars, while her accomplice went with hollowed-out batteries that he placed in flashlights. They each chose a secure and private location and then buried their shares once more.

By September, Schermeyer had grown impatient. He dug up his stashed money, pulled out a few small bills, and made some purchases of mundane supplies for the roadhouse. Then he waited to see if his actions generated any suspicion or investigation. If they did, he was prepared to claim that he had merely used some bills that recent lodgers at his roadhouse had left to pay their bill for a night's stay. When nothing came of it, he gained confidence and decided that his stay in Alaska had gone on long enough. It was time to head outside to kick up his heels while he still could.

In the fall of 1924, Schermeyer was almost seventy years old. He had never broken the law before—that is, if you don't count selling bootlegged whiskey to his roadhouse customers. But all the roadhouse operators did that; it was just a part of running that kind of establishment. It was good business. No, he had been a law-abiding Territorial citizen since his first days in the North Country in 1900, when he had arrived in Alaska to search for gold. He had moved on from the Klondike to the Fairbanks rush in 1904, and then sometime later to Kantishna, in the present-day Denali backcountry, to try his luck as a miner there. He eventually ended up in Iditarod by 1912.

Schermeyer was beginning to feel the pinch of age; hard winters put the hurt on many people's joints, causing aches and pains. He gave up on mining for gold and got into the roadhouse business during the winter months to serve dogsledders and other hearty, cold-weather travelers in need of a hot fire, a meal, and a warm bed. In the summer months he fared well growing vegetables in his greenhouse. Schermeyer was not poor by any means, but he was not getting rich either. By 1924, he felt it was time to sell out, take his legal and illegal gains, and head for warmer climes on the West Coast. He was tired of work and wanted a few years of fun before the end came.

Black Bear looked at the future differently. Although not yet a full-fledged legend of the Far North, many people in the Alaskan gold rush communities knew her personally, or had heard of her. Nellie Bates was one of thousands of women who either alone, with a spouse, or with a partner had traveled north to find fortune, to accompany men, to escape an unsatisfying existence in the States, or to take advantage of perceived opportunities.

In the traditional narratives of the gold rush era, men have dominated the focus of historians. In the popular myth, rugged male individualists confronted natural and man-made dangers in an epic quest for gold and furthering America's progress. Women, if they entered into this pageant, served mainly as exotic, or even erotic, accessories to the main storyline of hardship and struggle that came to symbolize Western American expansion. Certainly the rugged, individualistic men of the Far North lived lives worthy of note, but women represented only 10 percent of the "stampeders" who made their way to the gold fields of Alaska. Still, they took their place alongside the men and faced the same hardships and obstacles, such as the journey over the mountains to the Klondike, or the brutal reality of travel by dogsled through the Alaskan Interior at 50 below.

Contrary to the general view, not all of these women were prostitutes. Most of them found that the gold was not easy to come by, and they had to rely on their wits and work ethic to get by. Women of all ages, single or divorced, married or widowed—all those willing to meet the challenges and to work hard—often found excellent opportunities to not only get by, but to get ahead.

Experienced in cooking, sewing and washing clothing, and cleaning, women found their skills in high demand in the gold camps and towns of Alaska. Men were willing to pay top dollar for these services. Many women got their start in a restaurant or laundry and soon found themselves in a position to hang out a shingle as proprietors of their own establishments. Professional women also came north to work in offices, public and private, for newspapers, and as teachers and nurses. Women also staked claims to their own mines, bought and sold claims and real estate, and ran larger-scaled mining operations that hired laborers to do the work.

Of course, times were tough for many men and women who were lured north by the hope and promise of a better life. Oftentimes, those down on their luck found that life did not get any easier for them in the North. The popular view of fallen women, or "soiled doves" in Alaska's gold rush history, seems rather romantic. In local days of commemoration in the early twenty-first century, gold rush–era prostitutes are always portrayed as good-time women, the prostitutes with hearts of gold, living a free and fun-loving life, providing companionship and love, for a price, to the lonely prospectors. In this wildly unrealistic image, the oldest profession looks innocent, fun, and lucrative. Fabulously attired women spent their time having rich and boisterous gold seekers buy them drinks in crowded bars, fight over them, and queue up to have earthy fun with them.

More recently, historians have questioned this popular view to remind us that the American frontier always comprised a complex and often tangled mix of attitudes and values. On the one hand, gold rush prostitutes are viewed with fascination, and with a tendency to emphasize the sensational and the erotic. Yet, on the other hand, modern-day prostitutes who ply their trade on the streets don't receive anywhere near the positive associations. Perhaps that is because people today can see the physical and psychological effects of this precarious existence on the faces of modern prostitutes, and in the grim statistics that underscore the reality of life on the streets: the drug and alcohol use, the violence, and the diseases, to mention a few.

Life was similar for many of the prostitutes of the gold rush era. They faced some of the grim realities of street workers in modern American cities. Prostitution was a vocation for many, but one that often encumbered their lives in ways that they neither controlled nor expected. Wide social acceptance on the frontiers of America for these women or their profession remained elusive. It certainly was not a glamorous lifestyle. Working day in and day out in a canvas tent with one dirty miner after another tended to be tedious, even monotonous, rather than fun and adventurous. Prostitutes tended to come from the poorest of frontier families; they turned to the profession at an early age, and lacked educational and vocational skills. These roots in poverty and ignorance were rarely transcended by such a vocation. Prostitutes often suffered economic and social deprivation for their entire lives. Most of them earned little money, in part because they earned their living by selling services to poor working-class men. Those who did secure decent financial windfalls often lacked the knowledge or ability to successfully manage such resources. It must be remembered that these women lived on the fringes of frontier society, and often experienced violence and the capricious nature of local legal authority. In sum, the legal system tolerated them as criminals working an illegal, if "necessary," vocation.

Nellie "Black Bear" Bates was the exception to the rule, however, and her remarkable story suggests that some women *did* build lives for themselves that transcended the pit of prostitution on the frontier. Forty-year-old Nellie Bates was an old hand at the world's oldest profession in 1922. She had worked mining camps and communities in Alaska since 1901. After two decades, Black Bear, as she was affectionately known by the miners, actually accumulated some capital to show for her hard work. She also proved herself a savvy businessperson over

A dogsled mail carrier leaving an Alaskan Interior village, c.a. 1915. *Rivenburg, Lawyer and Cora Photograph Album. 1994-70-168. Archives. Alaska and Polar Regions Collections. Rasmuson Library, University of Alaska, Fairbanks.*

the years, and earned a reputation for grubstaking miners at fair interest rates. Black Bear also invested her earnings in profitable mining ventures. The men who knew her liked her and respected her business acumen.

Unfortunately for Black Bear, one investment in a mine on Chicken Creek had recently lost $17,000, a tidy sum in the early 1920s. So she was hard at work at her trade, providing "company" for the lonely miners of a little town called Flat. She hoped to raise more money to invest, or perhaps to purchase a ticket on the next steamship down the Yukon and back to the lower forty-eight states. The losses took a toll on her psychologically, and she remained unsure about whether she could muster the stamina to continue on. She realized that her youth and vitality were rapidly fading. The "sporting life" remained a young woman's game, especially on the Last Frontier, a place so primitive and rugged that just getting through a winter day could exhaust the heartiest men and women.

One day in late November 1922, the mail carrier, Bill Duffy, arrived in Flat to make his delivery and rest his dogs for the return trip to McGrath and Nenana. He visited Black Bear and the other working girls for a few days. After thinking the matter through, Black Bear asked Bill if she could ride with him on his trip. She had decided that Seattle would be a welcome relief after twenty years of darkness, cold temperatures, and hard work on the Alaskan frontier. Another working girl, Nadine Saum, took a ride as well, hoping to get to Iditarod to try her luck there for a time. When the mail-sled dog team had rested up, the three packed their things and loaded onto the sled. Nadine bundled up to ride in the sled, Nellie rode the runners, and Bill ran by their side with the gee pole to direct the dog team.

Mushing on winter trails can be a bonding experience. Temperatures often drop to 50 below. In such conditions, small groups remain dependant on each other to survive the challenges of the weather, to note the changing trail conditions, and to guard the health of the dogs. Everyone had to work together to ensure the safety of the group. This trip went off without anything unusual happening. They camped a few nights out as they made their way toward Iditarod. At night around the fire, Bill told stories. The one that Black Bear liked the most was the one that revealed the contents of the canvas mail pouch tucked away on the sled. Bill could not resist that one!

A few months earlier, Dexter Horton Bank, a Seattle concern, had mailed $30,000 in currency to a McGrath man called Thomas Atkins. The money shipped out on a steamer in early

October to Seward, Alaska. From there, it was placed on a steam engine and rode the rails to Nenana. Once it arrived in Nenana, postal workers placed it on the mail sled. After a few weeks spent waiting for proper trail conditions, the dog team finally mushed off to make the 250-mile trek to McGrath. While the trails were finally ready for travel in late November, the mail team—a relay team of two sets of sleds, dogs, and drivers—was delayed twenty days when an inexperienced musher lost his way and had to backtrack to find the right trail.

The mail finally got through, but once it arrived in McGrath, a new problem arose. The postmaster in McGrath did not have a key to open the mail bag. Bill Duffy, the experienced mail carrier of the relay team, found himself carrying the McGrath mail pouch with him all the way to the end of his line: Flat. Postal authorities told Duffy to hold on to the pouch until he found a postmaster with the right key to open it. The postmistress of Flat possessed the right key and opened the bag. This gave Duffy an opportunity to satisfy his curiosity about the contents of the troublesome mail bag. The Flat postmistress then instructed Duffy to drop the pouch off in McGrath on his return trip.

Imagine trying to keep that secret to yourself in the presence of two women on a lonely, frozen, and dark Alaskan trail. Duffy could not resist the temptation. So, he told Black Bear and Nadine about the saga of the canvas mail pouch, right up to the point where they entered into the story. Here he was, Duffy told them, on his way back to McGrath with a whole lot of cash.

Black Bear liked the story. In fact, she could not stop thinking about it on the trail. Maybe her efforts to escape the Far North had been a little too hasty after all?

The trio kept working the dogs and the sled on the trail, finally making Iditarod after several more days of hard work. Once there, Nadine said good-bye to them. Now it was only Nellie and Bill on the sled. They stopped 16 miles out of Iditarod at a roadhouse operated by Bill Schermeyer. Weeks earlier, Black Bear had invited friends from the surrounding districts to come wish her bon voyage on her trip to Seattle. There was a good crowd of well-wishers there to greet her, and soon the bootlegged booze began to flow and spirits began to soar.

Bill Duffy joined in on the merriment. He left the mail pouch on the sled without any concern for the large stacks of cash on board. Everyone knew each other at the party, so Duffy believed there was no need to distrust them.

The party inside Schermeyer's roadhouse raged into the long Alaskan winter night. Nellie had not been drinking as much as her friends, but kept up appearances nonetheless. She finally cornered the proprietor of the roadhouse in a quiet nook and popped a question to him. By this time, word of Bill Duffy's cargo had spread far and wide. He had told the story to several people in Flat before he'd left that community, and they had done the rest.

Indeed, Schermeyer knew what Duffy carried on his sled even before Black Bear brought it up. She simply asked Schermeyer if he was game to make some money that night. It was a vague comment, but he got the point. He smiled and answered affirmatively. That was all the two new partners in crime needed to say to each other.

The guests continued with their libations and card games into the night. Nellie used their distractions to slip away from the party for a few moments. She went outside to the barn where the dog team slept. Her heart was racing, and she looked about repeatedly to ensure that no one witnessed her actions. She quietly patted the exhausted dogs to keep them quiet. She need not have worried. After days spent with her on the trail, her presence was not enough to stir the exhausted animals from their blissful slumber.

Nellie grabbed the canvas money bag from the McGrath mail pouch and stashed it under her dress. She walked back toward the main building, but stopped at Schermeyer's fish cache, a small shed-like structure suspended by four large poles about fifteen feet off the ground. Alaskans used these structures to store food in a manner that made it accessible only to humans by a pole ladder. It was the best way to keep bears and other camp robbers out of the smoked and frozen meats.

Nellie climbed up the ladder and opened up the cache. She barely noticed the strong fish smell that wafted lazily out of the structure in the frozen air. She shoved the bag in under some fish, carefully made her way down the ladder, and went back to the roadhouse to mingle with her well-wishers. When she got inside her heart was pounding. She was exhilarated by the ease with which she had carried out her act of theft. She made eye contact with Schermeyer. He made no response, but understood the signal.

The rest was left to him. Schermeyer's role in this heist was to take the pouch and hide it in a secure spot until the heat of the thievery died down and it was safe to use the money. Schermeyer went out to the cache after the last of the revelers had finally passed out. It was morning, but still dark near the Arctic Circle. He harnessed his dogs to a sled, grabbed the bag, and mushed his team down the trail from his roadhouse out into the frozen bush. He found a good location up on a little knoll with good drainage and buried the sack in the snow. Then he drove his dog team over the site repeatedly to remove all signs of his burial activities.

Satisfied with his work, Schermeyer noticed for the first time that day the stirrings of hunger. He got his dog team back on the trail home and then mushed them back to the roadhouse to get breakfast on the griddle before his hungover guests woke up.

That spring, at breakup, Schermeyer retrieved the money bag and stashed it close to his greenhouse operation in Iditarod. The postal investigation remained ongoing. Consequently, neither he nor Black Bear felt comfortable using any of the currency. On one occasion, Black Bear somehow discovered that a postal inspector was headed out to Schermeyer's place for an interview with the man who ran the roadhouse where the money had been lost.

Black Bear descended into a state of panic and raced out to warn her accomplice and to make sure that the money was well hidden. Schermeyer felt uneasy about the burial spot and decided that the inspector would look all over his grounds if he became the least bit suspicious. So, he moved the hiding place again, this time to his garden, where he dug a hole deep enough, he felt, to prevent discovery.

Later that September, Schermeyer dug up the money again, just in case. He was concerned that he had buried the bag too deep. If they needed to move out in a hurry during the winter, they might run into trouble breaking through the rock-hard frozen ground. This time he stuck the bag of money under a few tons of carrots in his root house. There it stayed until the next spring, when the two coconspirators decided to check on it once more.

It took them several days to find it again, but once they did, they discovered that all the bills were now wet. They spent several nerve-racking days locked in his house, ironing the bills and hanging them out to dry. All the while Schermeyer stood guard. When that task was finally completed, the two carefully placed the bills into mason jars and dug a hole out in the field. After the thaw, Schermeyer dug up the loot one more time and buried it in the ground under his barn. The stress had finally caught up to them both. They agreed to just lay low, but that was a sentiment easier said than done for the two jumpy novice criminals. They knew in their rational minds that a little investment in time would pay great dividends later, and potentially keep them out of trouble with the law. But fear and panic kept creeping in from the more primitive parts of their brains. Somehow they remained patient for another year, until 1924.

By the summer of that year, they both felt that things had quieted down with the investigation. Schermeyer dug up the money for the last time—he had hidden it in so many different locations over the last year that he had lost count! When nothing more was heard from investigators, he grew more confident. He and Black Bear met to dry the money and divide up the spoils of their heist. Schermeyer used a few of the bills in town on some minor purchases, and then sat back for several weeks to see what, if anything, would come of it.

Nothing! Schermeyer started to make some plans. He was no longer a young man. It seemed that now was as good a time as any to finally make the great trek south to retire in the States. It seemed to him that he had spent a lifetime at heavy work in Alaska. He liquidated his assets in Iditarod and prepared to head Outside.

Right before Schermeyer took passage, Black Bear came to him once again in a fit of fear. She informed him that Bill Duffy, the mail-team driver, had become suspicious of them and had accused them of the theft. He wanted to cut a deal with them in exchange for his silence. Black Bear pleaded with the old man to cooperate with her on the deal. By this time, old Schermeyer wanted no trouble. He just wanted to get out of Alaska and live out the rest of his days in relative leisure. He agreed to give Duffy a portion of his share of the loot to keep him quiet. It was $4,000 worth of insurance!

Schermeyer first traveled to Eugene, Oregon. While he resided in that small city he ran into hard luck. An illness incapacitated him for some time. Perhaps all of the stress from the heist and trying to lie low had taken a toll on him. It had been difficult for him to sleep on many nights as his imagination and fear of discovery repeatedly got the best of him. His nerves had been about shot before he finally made his escape from the Last Frontier.

Things got so bad for him that he rented a room in Eugene and hired a private nurse. Alas, it appeared that the woman was not much of a nurse after all, but had used all her womanly charms to gain his confidence. He did regain his health, but the nurse decided to help herself to $1,000 in diamonds that Schermeyer had purchased with his stolen money. He took her to court and charged her with theft, but she was able to beat the charge and keep the diamonds. Easy come, easy go.

Schermeyer took the geographic cure and kept heading south all the way to San Diego, hoping to escape from his troubles, and perhaps a guilty conscience as well. There he took up with a prostitute and her friend. The three spent a great deal of time together, often crossing into Mexico to go to the track to watch the horse races on a daily basis. Before long, he discovered that those two wenches had taken money from him too.

Schermeyer decided it was time to take stock. His leisurely retirement plan had not panned out as he had expected. Indeed, he discovered that he was nearly broke. What to do, he thought, until he finally hit upon an idea. It was a long shot, but he had nothing to lose. He wrote to his former partner in crime, Black Bear, and told her of his run of bad luck with the dishonest women of the Outside World. Could she find it in her heart to take pity on an old friend and fellow Alaskan and send him a little spending money? Perhaps enough to get back on his feet, he pleaded. It would be just a loan, he added. Maybe $500?

Black Bear had been experiencing a run of bad luck of her own. She responded to three plaintive inquiries from Schermeyer. Each time she told him that she could not help out. Seeking to place the blame on others, Schermeyer told himself that he should have known better than to have trusted prostitutes!

Schermeyer was grieved to discover that his old accomplice had become so cold. But there was little he could do, so he decided to head for Los Angeles for a visit and to see if he could change his luck for the better. Again, things didn't work out the way he had hoped. While he was there, postal inspectors caught up with him. It would seem that he had attracted their attention when he took his former nurse to court in Oregon to try to get his diamonds back.

The story had made the local papers. The inspectors caught wind of it and began to put two and two together. They had been trying to track him down ever since. They asked him if he would speak to them and answer a few of their questions. The old man could hardly say no under the circumstances. In fact, he had grown tired of running, and decided that it was time to face the consequences of his actions, own up to his part of the caper, and seek some kind of redemption and peace in his last years. More to the point, he was angry at Black Bear and agreed to testify against her!

U.S. Marshal Lynn Smith of Fairbanks traveled to Los Angeles at government expense to accept Schermeyer's confession to the crime, arrest him, and personally supervise his return to Alaska. Smith was the marshal at Flat at the time of the heist in January 1923, and had a personal stake in the outcome of the trial against Black Bear. He also knew the Territory's star witness on a personal level. He actually liked Schermeyer and thought that it was best for him to turn Territorial witness because he would get a better deal from the government on his own charge.

Smith felt bad for the old man. Sure, he had sold bootlegged booze at his roadhouse, but he was essentially an honest businessman. The fact that Smith blamed the entire incident on Black Bear and viewed the prostitute as having coerced the old-timer into doing something he would not have ordinarily done suggested that he embraced the double standard held against women in the North, especially those involved in prostitution. Black Bear had caught Schermeyer at a weak moment, Smith believed, after she had already launched her plan, and then she kept the pressure on him. Before he knew what had really happened, the poor old guy found himself already implicated in the crime. Had he had time to sleep on her offer to be an accomplice, Smith assured himself, the old-timer surely would have steered clear of getting himself involved in such a dirty deed. Such was the view of constituted authorities in Alaska. Justice was blind, indeed!

Black Bear was put on trial in Fairbanks in early 1926. She flatly denied having anything to do with the theft. With the help of Tom Marquam, who served as legal council for the defense, Black Bear poked holes in Schermeyer's testimony, pointing out that there was absolutely no direct evidence that tied her to the crime outside of the Territorial witness who claimed to be merely her accomplice. There was only Schermeyer's word and anecdotal evidence that Black Bear was spending more money than she earned. Just how the prosecution determined the income of a prostitute who was working in a black-market economy and illegal industry was not explained.

The toughest obstacle that the prosecution had to overcome was the statute of limitations on prosecuting theft. It was too late to do anything about Black Bear's possible connection to the initial crime of stealing the money. The only thing that the Territory could hope to get her on was taking a share of the ill- gotten loot. On that line they had no hard evidence.

It was a poorly conceived, even desperate case brought by the government. The jury was hung. But that did not stop the prosecution from bringing a new case against the defendant a few weeks later. The second time was not a charm for the government, and the jury brought back a verdict of not guilty. Officials at the Postal Service complained that the jury, comprised as it was of Alaskans, was not fit, and had allowed the defendant to get away with the crime because they did not like the government and she had not hurt anyone.

There may have been something to these suspicions. The defense attorney, Marquam, had emphasized the strength, power, and monetary resources brought to bear by the government in their case against his client. Indeed, it was an almost brutal array against Black Bear that included three Justice Department attorneys, several inspectors connected to the U.S. Postal Service, and a small army of government agents, all carrying boxes of official documents that they claimed implicated the defendant.

Of course, it was still not a fair fight. Despite the image he created of a poor defenseless woman, the fact of the matter was that Nellie "Black Bear" Bates had many friends in Fairbanks and throughout the mining communities of the Interior. She was now living with Bill Duffy, the man who had run the postal dogsled team at the time of the theft. The two of them had been tipped off that Black Bear was going to be charged with the crime. They quickly went from Flat to Fairbanks ahead of the grand jury indictment, which would lead to her arrest and being held in jail for the duration of the trial. The two of them looked up all their old friends from her gambling and prostitution days. They reminded their friends and acquaintances that Black Bear had been a prostitute with a heart of gold who had helped out many miners who were broke or otherwise down on their luck. She had loaned money and grubstaked many of them. This little public relations campaign probably helped, given the fact that the jury would comprise people that either knew Black Bear personally or knew of her and her story.

Hers was a story that the old-timers were proud to tell. It was a story of the rugged Far Northern Frontier. And around these parts, by God, Black Bear was a true sourdough heroine. She took on a large federal bureaucracy and won fair and square in their eyes!

In the end, Schermeyer was the only one who ever served time for the crime: a year in jail. He died shortly after his sentence was over. Black Bear married Bill Duffy to become an honest woman. Many thought that he had probably been involved in the crime all along, but there was nothing to do but smile about it at that point. In the end, the government had spent several times more money than had been stolen trying to investigate the crime and then prosecute the alleged perpetrator. That thought must have stirred the heart of Black Bear as she contemplated her luck and her pluck!

Thomas Johnson:
The Blueberry Kid

Thomas Johnson, the Blueberry Kid, may have loved to eat wild blueberries when he worked as a steam hoist operator on a Cleary Creek mine near Fairbanks, but he was no kid. His fellow workers at the mine described him as a man in his mid-forties in 1912. That was the year that he allegedly murdered John Holmberg, Marie Schmidt, and Frank Adams. The "Kid," it seemed, was in fact a serial killer in the Territory of Alaska.

In the late summer of 1912, Johnson owned and operated a steam launch called the *Seal Pup* on the upper Koyukuk River, a major tributary of the Yukon River that drew its waters largely from the Brooks Range in Northwest Alaska. It was rugged country as far as Alaskan prospectors were concerned. Small camps with names such as Coldfoot dotted the river and underscored the challenges posed by the climate to those who sought mineral wealth from the region's surface and subsurface.

Athabascan peoples knew the area as a tough place to make a subsistence living. Fish provided their main source of sustenance, since large game like moose and other fur-bearing animals remained relatively scarce in this district. By the early twentieth century, the central economic activity came from mining, followed by jobs in the service fields, created by the mining industry.

While most non-Natives who ventured into the Koyukuk country scratched out a subsistence living, a few managed to earn small fortunes. John Holmberg, for example, came north in 1897 during the Klondike rush. He spent more than a decade prospecting throughout the Yukon Territory and into Alaska, where his luck changed in 1909 near the mining community of Wiseman on the Koyukuk.

He staked a claim on the Hammond River and spent the winter by himself, digging a shaft through the permafrost to bedrock, about 150 feet. By the spring of 1910, he struck pay dirt and began to extract significant amounts of gold. Two years later, Holmberg had made good money, and was ready to leave the cold winter conditions on the Koyukuk for the easy living in the States. He leased out his claim for $50,000 and booked passage down the Koyukuk on the Kid's launch.

Accompanying Holmberg on this trip was his fiancée, a woman called Marie Schmidt, or "Dutch Marie." Holmberg and Dutch Marie went back many years to his days as a prospector in the Klondike near Dawson City. A working girl at the time, Dutch Marie had busily compiled her own little fortune before Holmberg hit it big. The two spent many a carefree hour together and fell in love over time. Dutch Marie continued to work her trade, but she did follow Holmberg to Alaska. When he hit the big gold seam, he talked her into retiring and going south with him to Seattle.

One other traveler had booked passage on the *Seal Pup* that September. Frank Adams had spent many years in the Far North, mainly as a laborer, but occasionally as a prospector. He did not enjoy much success in any venture, unlike his two traveling partners. His luck was about to go from bad to worse, and it would rub off on Holmberg and Schmidt, as well.

Johnson worked the Koyukuk and Yukon rivers all summer during the season of 1912. He had hoped to make some good pay off his launch, ferrying people and freight up and down these major waterways of the Interior. But by the time he had paid his operating costs and other debts, Johnson was surprised and disappointed to have only about $700 left. That was not much to show for a long season of work. It must have proved frustrating to carry two relatively wealthy passengers, especially because Holmberg could not resist bragging about his good fortune, perhaps even revealing that he carried $8,000 on his person.

Johnson wanted that fortune. He was the kind of man who would do anything to get it. That desire, coupled with the remoteness of the Koyukuk—and the fact that no one would miss the passengers if they disappeared in this vast and remote part of Alaska—meant trouble.

Johnson was a man of somewhat mysterious origins. He reportedly came from Yarmouth, England, but no one knew that for a fact. In the early 1890s he had worked in Seattle as a smuggler on a sloop that he operated in Puget Sound. Things eventually got a little too dodgy there, so he worked his way up north to Wrangle, Alaska. There he took a job as an engineer on a tugboat for a salmon cannery.

In Wrangle he fancied a young Tlingit woman called Mary and took her for his wife. He failed, however, to follow the custom of the country in this marriage when he did not provide the young woman's family with the full bride price. Johnson gave her stepfather only $50 of the $250 that he had agreed to pay. The Tlingit man set out to collect what was due his family according to their tradition. He confronted Johnson. Johnson agreed to pay up, but clearly did not intend to be parted from his money for long. Johnson allegedly killed his new wife and then tracked her parents down to the beach, took back his bride payment, and killed them too. Then he dragged their canoe up into the forest to hide the deed.

No one ever saw Mary or her family again. Most likely, Johnson disposed of their bodies in the ocean. Their canoe was eventually discovered hidden in the thick brush near the shore. The only other evidence ever discovered by the authorities looking into the disappearance of the three Tlingits was the charred remains of some clothing said to have belonged to Mary's mother. The stepfather was known to have been carrying a little over $200, and the mother to have worn a necklace made of large gold nuggets. Johnson left Wrangle immediately after their disappearance. The authorities never charged Johnson or anyone else with a crime, in part because there was no evidence, no dead bodies, and the victims were Natives.

Johnson drifted down to South America where he took up work in the large-scale Panama Canal project then under way.

A steam launch pilot and his dog on the lower Yukon River in 1926. *Alaska State Library, George A. Parks Photographs, P240-239.*

He spent a few years down there working on a donkey engine before he eventually made his way back north to Alaska in 1908. It was here that he took the job on Cleary Creek operating a steam hoist. The work did not agree with him, and he rushed with many others to the diggings on the Iditarod. He just managed to scratch out a living there as well. It frustrated him to work so hard and live in an isolated land and rugged climate, and all seemingly for naught. Why did fate smile upon others and pass over him?

Johnson soon gave up on the Iditarod and purchased the *Seal Pup*. He piloted his new boat to the Yukon River and made his way up to the Koyukuk country. Toward the end of the 1912 season he took stock of his earnings and the work that he had done. The two did not match his expectations.

He was on the upper Koyukuk, near Wiseman, during the second week of September. He was pondering his situation when Holmberg and the others requested passage to Nulato, a trading center on the lower Yukon River. They thought it fortuitous that Johnson had arrived with the *Seal Pup* when he did. Securing passage on northern rivers at this time of year was always tenuous. Failure meant either hunkering down for a long winter or braving winter travel in a dogsled. Neither choice appealed to the three. From Nulato they planned to book passage to St. Michael on one of the regular steamboats that plied that river until freeze-up closed down the main water highway to shipping traffic for the winter. At St. Michael they could book tickets on a steamship to Seattle.

Johnson and his three passengers began the trip downriver with nothing out of the ordinary to report. At about 70 miles before the confluence of the Koyukuk with the Yukon, however, the *Seal Pup* made an unexpected stop. Johnson headed up a blind slough a fair piece and then stopped. The passengers must have wondered what had happened when they realized they were no longer on the main river channel. What happened next only Johnson could say. Perhaps he told the curious passengers that he needed to take on firewood for his boiler, or that he needed a rest. From the scanty evidence collected during the subsequent years, it appeared that Johnson did not leave his passengers guessing for too long. Somehow, he killed them, probably in their sleep, took their gold and money, and then scuttled his boat in the slough. From there he walked out and caught a ride on the next launch coming down the river to Nulato.

Once he made Nulato, Johnson hired himself out on the *J. P. Light* and worked his way down the Yukon to St. Michael, where he purchased passage to Seattle in steerage on the SS *Victoria*. This vessel left on October 8, 1912. Always calculating an angle, Johnson organized a raffle ticket sale on board the *Victoria* for the other passengers and crew. The prize was a large gold nugget and a brooch made of walrus ivory. Alice Stewart won the brooch; sources don't say who won the nugget.

After his arrival in Seattle on October 16, the Kid lived the high life during his short two-day stay in the "Queen City." He dropped about $100 each day at the ritzy Hotel Victoria, at the saloon on First Avenue operated by Jack O'Neil, and in riding about town in automobiles. Johnson also conducted some business affairs that later caught the interest of the authorities. At the U.S. Assay Office, he traded in some gold dust for just over $2,000 in paper bills. He also traded gold to Jack O'Neill, worth another $3,500.

Visitors from the Far North were in great demand in Seattle at the turn of the twentieth century. Since the Klondike rush of 1897, the city had grown from about 75,000 in that year to just over 237,000 people by 1910, as a result of its status as the "Gateway to Alaska." Throngs of people came from across the country to use the city as their staging ground for the great trek north. An equally large group of people returned from their northern exposure to spend their hard-earned—or, in Johnson's case, ill-gotten—fortunes and to spin tales of their experiences.

The constant traffic to and from Alaska passing through Seattle stoked a fascination among the local residents for this exotic destination. Not only was it good business for this boom-and-bust West Coast city, but the adventure could be experienced vicariously through the tales told by the sour-doughs on their return. Even the rich and famous got caught up in the romance. Men such as Jack London and Wyatt Earp stayed in the bustling business district of Pioneer Square, with its colorful cast of characters working and playing "below the line" among the docks, bars, hotels, parlor houses, crib houses (low budget houses of prostitution), hash houses, pawn shops, dope houses, gambling dens, and restaurants. This was a wild district indeed. Authorities tolerated the parlor houses, with their infamous madams, because they operated as legitimate businesses. Crib houses, such as the Paris, were controversial public nuisances and health hazards. They were operated by thugs and were downright dangerous, several of them containing as many as 100 tiny rooms. Police feared to enter this district individually.

It was a high time indeed. Johnson took in the sights and smells of the city, but he quickly moved on to the gem of the

West Coast, San Francisco, where he arrived on October 21. He landed at the famous "Barbary Coast" district, which was home to the lowest, meanest, and vilest people of the city. It was, according to a Warren Commission Report in the 1930s, the home of drunks, prostitutes, gamblers, intoxicated rowdies, opium dens and denizens, disease, debauchery, misery, profanity, and death. It emerged during the gold rush when men from around the world entered into California through San Francisco. As the city burgeoned with new arrivals, a hard-core segment of the newcomers began to stake claim to real estate near the docks, where they set up shanties that offered cheap dates with working women, and cheap booze—including drinks spiked with laudanum. It was especially dangerous for sailors as a place where they were often "shanghaied." They would be out drinking, black out, and then wake up on a strange ship with a new kind of hangover from a drug slipped into their beverage.

From this misfits' paradise, the Kid then walked up from the docks and booked a room at the Stanford Hotel in the Tenderloin District. Located near the financial center of San Francisco, this residential neighborhood was a step up from the Barbary Coast, but offered similar if more upscale amenities, including gambling, billiards, boxing, theaters, bars, brothels, and restaurants. Vice, graft, and corruption thrived here, but it was a higher class or a more sophisticated kind of criminal operating here. After he conducted business with the U.S. Mint, where he exchanged gold worth nearly $7,000, the Kid headed down to the Tenderloin District to throw his money around and have a high time.

By all estimates, the Kid enjoyed himself with his ill-gotten riches. From this point, however, the trail grows as cold as the Alaskan tundra in January. It seems that his documented whereabouts end after he spent a few weeks in San Francisco. Where he went and what he did next became a mystery in part because no one knew that Johnson's victims were missing for more than a year after they had disappeared.

The effort to track down the perpetrator of this crime got off to a rather late start even by Alaskan standards. No one missed Holmberg, Schmidt, or Adams. Apparently, not even Adams's wife knew that he had attempted to leave Alaska in the fall of 1912. So, Territorial officials did not know that they should be tracking down a cold-blooded murderer and thief until a year later, in 1913.

It wasn't until late summer that people began to ask questions. First Adams's wife began to wonder why she had heard nothing from her husband for so long. Then, local Wiseman Deputy Marshal E. P. Heppenstall began to hear locals on the Koyukuk asking why Holmberg had neglected his interests there. He made contact with Louis Erwin, the U.S. marshal in Fairbanks.

After looking into matters briefly in the Interior, Erwin engaged outside help in Seattle to conduct an inquiry on that end while he started an investigation on the Koyukuk and Yukon rivers. He cabled Special Agent Joseph Warren, who served as Alaska's judicial representative in the Seattle area. Warren immediately began to look into the Alaska Steamship records to learn who had traveled from St. Michael in the fall of 1912. He tracked down and interviewed witnesses. His investigation revealed that Johnson had traveled from the north to San Francisco.

Warren also identified a few witness leads in Idaho and in Alaska, but because of the late start of the investigation, none of them ever panned out. In May 1914, Warren gave an interview to reporters from several large newspapers serving the Pacific Northwest. Even though official charges had not been made, and there were no dead bodies or other evidence of foul play, he named Johnson as the perpetrator of the crime.

Meanwhile, new clues and leads began to surface in Alaska. A woman called Mrs. J. K. Smart, living in Fairbanks, reported to authorities that she had talked to Johnson, an old friend, in the Yukon Territory town of Whitehorse in 1913. When asked if she could be mistaken, she said that there was no way; she knew Johnson well, and did not mistake him for another man. Of course, it had been so long since she had seen him that the information was practically useless. It did, however, lead to some speculation on the possibility that the Kid had made his way from the Canadian side back into Alaska to raid Holmberg's secret cache on the Koyukuk River. The dead man had hidden 450 ounces of gold there, reputed to be worth about $10,000.

Another potential break in the case came from Koyukon Indian villagers, who had discovered the scuttled *Seal Pup* in the spring of 1913. It would have perhaps been useful information had the authorities thought to ask the Natives in the region if they had seen or heard anything of the missing people. It wasn't until a year later that an investigator would question them. In June 1914, more than two years after the alleged murders, Captain George Green of the *Reliance* was led to Johnson's scuttled launch.

The find turned out to be anticlimactic. There was no proverbial smoking gun, although two Winchester rifles were found on board with a few personal articles and clothing. There were no bodies and no signs of any crime. The only useful information discovered centered on the fact that the boat had clearly been intentionally sunk. The engine still ran and the hull was sound.

Another Koyukon Indian community, Mountain Village, discovered the body of a woman in the late summer of 1914 on the Yukon River. It washed ashore a few hundred miles downstream from where Johnson had scuttled his launch. The Indians buried the decomposed body on a riverbank and notified authorities. When investigators came to exhume the body to perform an autopsy, the villagers told them that they were too late. High water in the preceding weeks had washed away the riverbank grave. Although the Indians looked for the body downriver for many days, they failed to find it.

The investigation grew ridiculous at times, such as when the deputy marshal from Iditarod, without orders or jurisdiction, traveled to the location of the scuttled boat to conduct his own investigation. J. J. Donovan claimed that he found evidence of the killings after only a fortnight's investigation. About 10 miles up from the slough where the Koyukon Indians had found the *Seal Pup*, Donovan claimed that he found a nugget of gold, a bullet, and the charred remains of human bones at an old campsite. He identified the bones on the spot as the remains of Frank Adams.

Alaskan authorities officially engaged in the investigation paid no attention to Donovan's claims. They knew that the deputy marshal from Iditarod was a close friend of Adams. They also knew that the missing man's widow held a $5,000 life insurance policy that remained unpaid for the lack of a body.

On September 12, 1914, two years to the day since Holmberg, Schmidt, and Adams had begun their trip down the

Koyukuk, two more deputy marshals, George Berg and J. L. Anders, began their trek to the upper Koyukuk for another crime-scene investigation. They returned about three weeks later with no information to contribute. The investigation remained open into the summer of 1915. Berg went back up the Koyukuk and broadened the area of his search. Remarkably, he discovered human bones of a man, eyeglasses that had belonged to Holmberg, and articles of women's clothing identified as belonging to Schmidt.

On August 3, 1915, an Alaska Territorial grand jury concluded that enough evidence of a crime existed. The grand jury charged Thomas Johnson for the murder of three people. It had been almost three years since the victims and Johnson had disappeared.

Friends of Johnson felt that he had also been murdered along with the others. They did not believe Johnson capable of committing such a crime. They needn't have worried about the Kid, though. Officials still had no clue as to his whereabouts. There were some rumors circulating that after a few weeks of libations and frolicking with the comfort girls of the Tenderloin District, the Kid had left the area for the Midwest, to recover.

In truth, investigators could only speculate on the Kid's whereabouts. In addition to the Midwest theory, some officials thought that he may have returned to England. Of course, this idea remained problematic because no one could demonstrate with any certainty that he had indeed come from that country originally. Special Agent Warren advanced a theory that the Kid had actually been murdered and robbed by thugs in the Tenderloin District. Johnson's friends recalled that the Kid occasionally talked about his desire to leave behind the cold climes and waters of the Far North for the islands of the South Sea. Maybe he had finally acted on his plan to purchase a vessel for trade in that tropical region.

As the case grew even colder, officials began to feel the pinch of the burgeoning expenses and the sting of minimal results. They finally closed the case in 1923. In 1938, a federal judge dropped the murder charges against Johnson. A U.S. attorney argued in 1937 that the former suspect would have been in his mid- to late sixties by that point, if he was still alive. Moreover, there were no witnesses left to be called, and the evidence was too meager to make a successful case against him in court. If Johnson was paying attention, he told no one. Indeed, no one ever saw him again.

Joe Horner, aka Frank Canton

"Damn you, Canton, I've got it in for you!" yelled Bill Dunn, a wanted outlaw in the Oklahoma Territory. It was November 6, 1896, in Pawnee, Oklahoma, and Frank Canton, a deputy marshal for Judge Isaac Parker in the Territory, had been on Dunn's trail for some time. Canton instinctively knew from years of experience that Dunn's call did not represent an idle threat. No; it meant business, and that bullets would soon fly.

Dunn had sworn earlier that if he ever got the chance he was going to gun Canton down. The moment he heard his name called out, Canton reflexively swung into action. It was life or death on the dirt streets and wooden boardwalks of Pawnee. Dunn, a quick draw and straight shooter, led a vertically integrated cattle-rustling outfit. The gang stole the cattle, butchered them, and then offered the meat for sale in legitimate shops. Occasionally they collaborated with the notorious Dalton Gang.

Canton was in town serving summonses to jurors for a session of the district court. He had let his guard down. Fortunately, he always carried his .45 caliber Colt revolver on his right hip. He had just walked out of a restaurant onto the boardwalk on a cold morning. He placed his hands in his pockets to warm them. With his head down, Canton started to cut a quick pace up to the courthouse when Dunn called him out.

Dunn had his hand on his holstered revolver when he spoke, but he never had a chance to draw it. Canton's reflexes, honed by a quarter-century of life-and-death experiences with guns, served him well on that crisp Oklahoma morning. He immediately drew his Colt, cocked it, and pulled the trigger in a lightning-quick and surprisingly fluid motion. The bullet struck Dunn in the center of the forehead. Before he even knew what had hit him, Dunn lay dead on the wooden sidewalk.

As a crowd of about a dozen men began to gather around the scene, Canton checked to make sure that Dunn was dead, and then walked over to Sheriff Lake's office to report the incident. Bill Dunn's brothers, upon hearing of the death of their brother, quickly saddled up their horses and rode out of town. Canton was not a man they wanted to mess with.

Yes, Canton was a cool customer when things got rough, but that night, alone with his thoughts, he must have experienced some horror regarding this close call, and knowing that he had sent another man to his grave. He had occasionally suffered horrible nightmares in the past, and often awoke, screaming wildly. Perhaps the faces of all the men he had killed flashed through his mind. It had all begun with the two buffalo soldiers he had fought in a Texas shoot-out in October 1874. That was the first time he had killed someone. Back then his name was Joe Horner.

Horner's parents had crossed the country from Virginia to Texas in the mid-1850s, when Joe was only a child. In his teens, Joe Horner became a cowboy and worked the herds on the trails that led from Texas to Kansas in the late 1860s. Those were rough and rowdy times for Horner. He met some crazy characters working the trail; mean and rough men with few scruples who lived only for the moment.

There was, Horner quickly learned, not much money to be made in running someone else's cattle. Cowboys were cheap labor from all walks of life. The future in that work for most men seemed grim. That explained why Horner fell in with some bad elements. By 1871, he had robbed his first banks and begun a short career of rustling cattle. He played this illegal game for several years without incident, until that time in Jacksboro, Texas, when those African-American cavalrymen had attempted to take him down. He survived that day after he took one soldier's life and wounded the other, but that is when the nightmares started.

He tried to ignore these incidents. Most men of courage deny, at least initially, that they might be having problems coping with violent experiences. Horner continued with his outlaw career until 1877, when he finally got caught robbing a bank in Comanche, Texas. Somehow he managed to escape from jail before his trial. He immediately rode out of Texas and hired on as a cowboy on a herd headed for Ogallala, Nebraska.

Along the trail, throughout the days and often sleepless nights, he pondered the path that he had taken in life. Horner realized that he was at a crossroads. Thoughts of his loving mother troubled him. She would be so disappointed in the person he had become. His conscience got the better of him, and he determined to reform. He chose the path of law and order. Upon arriving in Ogallala, he vowed to straighten out his life.

As a symbol of his reform, and to avoid the practical complications that his old name might possibly create, he took on the alias of Frank Canton. It was a name that he kept until his death in 1927. Joe Horner was gone; Frank Canton emerged in his place. The new man fearlessly defended right against the forces of lawlessness. No matter the odds, Canton determined to defend productive people against thieving thugs that sought to take their hard-earned property.

Canton took work as a detective in Wyoming for a powerful stockmen's association. His charge was to prevent cattle rustling and to help the large stock growers in their bid to clear the range of the small-time operators settling in Johnson County. Eventually he became the sheriff in Johnson County, and, later, the government made him a U.S. deputy marshal.

In April 1892, one of the most famous range wars in Western history broke out, and Canton was right in the middle of it. He became a regulator, one of fifty armed gunmen riding with Frank Wolcott under the employ of the stock growers' association. He participated in the infamous action against rustlers Nate Champion and Nick Ray. The regulators sent a burning wagon into the K. C. Ranch cabin where Champion and Ray had barricaded themselves. When the two came out with clothes smoking and guns blazing, regulators cut them down in a hail of bullets.

The incident had Canton seeing ghosts of the men in his sleep and waking up in cold sweats to his own screams. It was too much for his nerves to see brave men gunned down like that. Historians have raised questions about the motives of the regulators hired by the large cattle ranchers, and the guilt of Champion and Ray. It might be that Canton did not think that he was on the side of right in this incident. Perhaps he did not find the odds fair. In any event, he resigned his post, told the ranchers he was quitting the regulators, and headed for Oklahoma. It was there that he took work again as a U.S. deputy marshal and began confronting real outlaws, such as Bill Dunn.

Canton's story is a bit of a twist from the other vignettes in this tome, and from what readers of the Outlaw Tales series are used to. It is the story of an outlaw who reformed himself. It is about second chances and what-ifs. Horner was a vicious killer, thief, and thug, who, as Frank Canton, became a famous law enforcement officer on many Western frontiers.

Not the least of these was Alaska.

Canton's autobiography does not reveal his motives for leaving his wife and daughter behind in 1897 to take an appointment in Alaska as a U.S. deputy marshal. Perhaps the night terrors had returned after he shot down old Bill Dunn, and these incidents affected his relationships. Did he fear what he might do to his wife during one of his nighttime fits? Or did he feel shame when he cried like a baby in her presence as he tried to push away the horrible images of death so that he could sleep?

At the time, Alaska, more than double the size of Texas, had only one judge and one marshal. They were assisted by ten deputy marshals. Canton agreed to become one of these deputies. In addition, by 1897, with miners streaming into the Interior by the thousands, the federal government had sent troops to St. Michael near the Yukon River. It also provided a revenue ship to patrol the river and its navigable tributaries. Military officials scouted out places to establish posts. In 1899, Fort Egbert was established at Eagle, and, in 1901, Fort Gibbon was built at Tanana, located near the confluence of the Tanana and Yukon rivers.

U.S. Marshal James Shoup dispatched a deputy marshal to the Interior to be stationed at Circle beginning in 1897. There was one problem, though; the new deputy, J. J. Rutledge, got sidetracked in Dawson along the Canadian route. He spent months there pulling his Territorial salary while prospecting for gold with the other stampeders. Months passed before Shoup found out. Months more passed before he could get word back to Rutledge. The new deputy marshal claimed that there were no larger steamboats making the passage to the American side of the Yukon River to Circle. Rutledge also protested that he had been warned against taking a berth on a smaller vessel for fear that it might get caught in the freeze-up. Shoup called his bluff. He knew that thousands of men had made their way through the Canadian passage on the Yukon into Circle and other Interior destinations. He fired Rutledge and then immediately hired Frank Canton.

It was February 1898, and the government was keen to get an active, fearless, and aggressive man such as Canton into the Interior to enforce the law and interests of both government and business. Shoup knew that Canton cared about his work and could be counted on to get the job done right. Canton's steamer from Seattle, the *Cleveland*, did not make St. Michael, 80 miles east of the mouth of the Yukon, until September. The season was getting late and Circle was nearly 1,000 miles up the Yukon River. Nevertheless, Canton made his way upriver on a small steamboat called the *St. Michael*. By the time they had made it up to Big Minook Creek above the Tanana, Canton realized that it was time to winter over. They would continue to Circle in the spring.

And, while he was at it, he could do some prospecting with some friends he had made along the way. Canton and his partners built a sturdy and snug little cabin in the newly thriving little boomtown of Rampart. There had been gold discoveries on Little Minook Creek. Newly created Rampart boasted the largest population on the Yukon River, at least on the Alaska side. Canton was still about 800 miles from Circle as freeze-up neared.

A local Athabascan Indian called Minook, who had been educated at a Catholic mission on the Yukon, told Canton and his partners that his people had found large nuggets of gold on the headwaters of the Big Minook a few years earlier. The party was especially interested to learn that no one had prospected in the area since then. A local white trader called Al Mayo, one of the first Americans on the Yukon, gave them a similar story. Taken together, the word of these two influential men of the Alaskan Interior was considered gospel. A few nights later, as many of the members of the camp stood by a fire, men ran into camp to show off the gold they had found in Big Minook Creek. Now the entire camp knew about the Big Minook site.

That was all it took. Men in the camp scrambled to get supplies together; others simply stuffed their pockets full of what food they had on hand. It was 25 miles up the creek to where the discovery had been made. Although the weather showed signs of winter's approach, the prospectors made a mad dash. Canton started off with six other men in his group. They packed with care. Each of them carried about seventy-five pounds on their back. As they hiked out of camp, rain began to fall on them. Within a short time they each carried several pounds of water as well.

The men pushed through, however, eager to stake a claim before it was too late. It was rough going because there was no trail. They crossed the crooked creek several times; each time they dealt with icy cold water up to their waists. Still, they pressed on for two days and nights. On the third day as they neared their goal, wet autumn snowflakes began to fall heavily. Somehow, two men of the party got separated and went up the wrong canyon following a tributary. Canton and the other four pressed on, driven by gold fever.

They finally reached the steep gorge Minook had told them about. Snow continued to fall, but because the ground remained unfrozen, it melted almost as quickly as it fell. Travel became increasingly difficult. They finally halted to make camp for the third night. They got a fire going and thankfully began to warm up and dry out. Just as they felt comfortable, at midnight, the roaring began.

Each man knew instantly what that noise meant. The snow and rains that had fallen on the steep mountains in the gorge had created a flash-flooding torrent of water up in the canyon. That water was now heading right toward their campsite. They could not climb up the steep canyon walls. They could only retrace their path from earlier in the day. One problem presented itself, however. The water in the creek had been rising all day. What had been hip-deep water was now as much as thirty feet deep, or higher. The gorge had become a "raging torrent" of icy cold water. In the darkness of the night Canton and his partners contemplated their plight.

One of the men in the party, Frank Kress, a lumberjack from the Midwest, worked out a plan in his head during the early hours of the morning. As dawn approached, he presented it to his partners. Many large spruce trees grew along the banks of the creek. He believed that they could chop some down to use as bridges over the foaming rapids. Slowly they made their way back out, using this method. It took several days, but they eventually made it out. Along the way they found one of the two lost members of their party. The other man had died of exposure.

It had been a rough and deadly trip for Canton's group, but two men from another party had also died on this stampede. It took two weeks for Canton to get the stiffness out of his joints. He described it as the most difficult journey of his life. He looked at the bright side, though. Canton wrote that he had learned an important lesson that he never forgot. For the rest of his time in Alaska, he never again traveled without taking proper food, clothing, and equipment. He never suffered such privation again.

Canton experienced other adventures at Rampart during the winter of 1898, but he passed the test, survived his first Alaskan winter, and soon became a real sourdough. In April, as he sat in his cabin with a partner, a man pushed open their door and walked in. He took off his coat and pack, and then looked at both men and asked if they knew where he could find U.S. Deputy Marshal Canton.

They told him he was in luck and to take a seat, whereupon the man recounted a story about a steamboat on the Yukon called the *Walrus*. As captain of the vessel he had ordered the crew and passengers into winter quarters on the Yukon at freeze-up, about 70 miles below the Koyukuk River. His 150 passengers and a load of supplies were bound for Dawson in the Yukon Territory. Over the course of the winter some hard cases took control of the boat and the cargo. They now controlled the camp. The captain learned that in the spring the gang planned to take another vessel, the *Cora*, also in winter camp, and use it to transport the cargo up the Koyukuk. Once they went up that river, they planned to prospect for gold.

The captain now wanted Canton to come with him to the camp and restore the authority of law and help recover the stolen property. Canton smiled and leaned back in his chair to ponder the situation. He was the only constituted law officer on the Yukon for 1,800 miles, save for one U.S. commissioner located at Circle. He realized the scope of the undertaking and that he alone would have to face the gang. Canton had heard rumors about some of the bad men at this camp over the course of the winter. He believed that some of the outlaws were wanted men back in the States.

Still, Rampart seemed dull. Canton wanted some excitement, and he liked the odds! It would be one good law enforcement officer against a camp of bad men. He looked at the steamboat captain and told him that he would take the job, return with him to the camp, take charge until the ice went out on the Yukon, and then travel with him up to Circle. At Circle, 300 miles below Dawson, he would assume his post at the U.S. marshal's office. The captain looked at him and smiled. He knew that he had found a man of courage and quiet confidence.

Canton packed up his things, including his Winchester, Colt, and plenty of ammunition. The two men headed out the next morning. They made good time on the packed snow, and in a matter of days, they arrived at the *Walrus*'s winter camp. The passengers had built a large number of cabins from the spruce trees above what they thought represented the high-water line of the Yukon. Canton knew right away that they had made an error in judgment. Ice jams of forty feet and higher were common on the Yukon, which caused flooding at places that would ordinarily be deemed safe on other rivers.

Canton did not waste any time with that issue, however. He spied the *Walrus*, anchored at the mouth of a small side stream, and headed straight for it. He climbed on board, pushed open the door to the captain's room, unloaded his pack, took off his boots and parka, set his rifle down by the woodstove, sat down on a chair, and then loaded his pipe. The three men seated at a table playing cards looked both shocked and angry at the temerity of this stranger. Who did he think he was to barge in to "their" quarters unannounced and uninvited and proceed to make himself comfortable. The outlaws suspected something was amiss, but the stranger said nothing. He just sat there eyeballing them.

Canton saw that each man wore a holster with a revolver and ammo.

Finally, one of the outlaws, one Canton thought he knew from somewhere, and whom he described as "villainous-looking," asked him where he came from. Canton replied coolly that he was from upriver. The evil-looking man grew angry and asked loudly what Canton was doing there.

Canton calmly stated his name and his position, and informed the men in the room that he now commanded the steamship and the cargo by order of the owner and the captain. The three men stared at each other blankly for a moment in stunned silence. The biggest of the three, the villainous one, then stated that Canton must be crazy. The only law in the Far North was what the men made for themselves. He told Canton that he and his men had contracted with the company for passage to Dawson, but had been left on this little island for the entire winter. That situation caused them to lose valuable gold claims in the Klondike. They decided to recover their damages from the company by seizing the *Cora* and all the company property they could take for a journey up the Koyukuk River in the spring. He then looked Canton square in the eye and delivered a steely warning: If he wanted to stay alive, he had better shut up and steer clear of him and his men. They planned to kill the first man who interfered with their plans.

Canton remained calm and collected. He told them that he appreciated their advice, but that he had always been one to take care of himself. Canton then asked the big man how he thought he would be able to take the boat. The villain looked at Canton, moved his hand toward his gun, and replied that he possessed it already.

Canton had been watching the gun hand of his adversary from the corner of his eye from the moment he entered the room. As soon as he saw it drop for the butt of the pistol, Canton's hand flashed like lightning to his Colt. Before the outlaws could blink they were staring down the bore of Canton's cocked .45. Canton told the men to unbuckle their gun belts and place their weapons and cartridges on the table. Then he lined the men up against the wall and spoke of his desire to shoot them right then and there. The only thing that prevented it, he warned them icily, was the fact that the ground outside was too frozen to easily dig a hole for their miserable remains.

Nevertheless, Canton wanted them to know that he represented the United States Marshal's Office. He planned to enforce law and order in the camp. This was the only chance they would get from him. The next time things would not go so easy on them. Canton opened up the door and told them to leave. As the three men filed out, the evil-looking man gave him a look that Canton knew could only mean trouble. The deputy

Yukon River ice piled high on the bank during breakup in May c.a. 1910.
*Rivenburg, Lawyer and Cora Photograph Album. 1994-70-293. Archives. Alaska and Polar
Regions Collections. Rasmuson Library, University of Alaska, Fairbanks.*

marshal of Circle knew he would have to watch his back until
the ice went out on the river.

When Canton apprised the captain of his meeting with the
gang's ringleader, the captain grinned widely for a moment.
Then he remembered his hospitality and set about to cook
a grand meal for the new hero of the camp. Over dinner he
told Canton that the villain's name was Tom Barkley. Barkley
had organized the worst elements of the camp into a gang and
exerted great power over them and the rest of the camp.

The first thing the next morning after breakfast, Canton
hoisted a U.S. flag on the steamer's flagpole. The camp residents began to file out of their cabins to get a look at the flag,
the deputy marshal, and the notices that he had posted to

inform them of his intention to strictly enforce the law in the camp. Canton told the passengers that he would give those with stolen company property one opportunity to return it immediately or face arrest. Those who returned property were still accountable for their actions, he continued, but he understood that the captain favored leniency for those who cooperated. In the morning, more than a ton of stolen cargo was returned. But Barkley and his men, who did not attend the meeting, remained sullen.

For the most part, the rest of the camp—nearly 150 men from all over the U.S., and the world—was favorably disposed to law and order. Many good men in camp fully supported Canton and responded to his call for volunteers. Canton appointed and swore in twenty special deputies to help keep order in the camp.

Soon Canton received information that implicated Barkley and his men in the theft of valuable furs from the *Walrus*. He organized five of his deputies and raided Barkley's cabin early the next morning. They found silver gray fox, golden marten, and polar bear pelts. They caught the thieves by surprise in their nightshirts. Canton took the captives to the steamboat and presented them and the evidence to the captain. The ship's clerk identified the furs as belonging to the company.

Canton immediately selected twelve men from the camp to serve as a jury, one man as defense counsel, and one man as prosecutor. He then called for the court to be in session with himself acting as the judge. The trial lasted through the day and into the night. The jury found all three defendants guilty. The court fined Barkley $1,000, and required the other two men to pay $500 each. The court also returned the furs to the ship.

Since the winter camp did not have a jail, Canton released the men on their own recognizance until breakup in the spring. Canton knew that there was nowhere to go, and that the convicted men would not try to flee. With the restoration of law and order, the camp settled down.

When April finally arrived, the snow in the mountains began to melt. The ensuing runoff flowed from tributaries into the Yukon under the thick sheet of ice that had covered it since the previous October. Eventually the pressure of the runoff would cause the layer of ice to shatter. When this happened, the awesome event known as the breakup on the Yukon River would commence. River ice sheared with tremendous pressure and an eerie noise. Those who lived by the river knew the danger that breakup presented. The broken ice would begin to flow down the swollen river, which moved it with tremendous force.

Flowing ice on the river often jams up into dams fifty feet or higher. When this occurs, water backs up behind the dams to flood everything upriver. At some point the weight of this water becomes too much for the ice dams to bear. They eventually burst, and the force of the backed-up water as it breaks through the dam and comes thundering down devastates everything in its path. The process often repeats itself for days on end until the ice finally melts and the river stabilizes. When this finally occurs, river traffic can begin to flow again, and the river goes back to serving as the main highway into the Interior for the season.

The residents of the winter camp knew what to expect. They cut into the ice around the two boats; it was nearly eight feet thick. Once they had freed the vessels, they moved them to standing water in a protected pool.

While this work was being done, Canton noticed that Barkley was starting to act restless. The deputy marshal kept his eyes on the outlaw. It was during this period of close observation that he finally realized Barkley's identity. The State of Idaho wanted him dead or alive for the heinous murder of three people. Barkley had committed this murder by dropping dynamite down an occupied mine shaft in the Coeur d'Alene mines of Northern Idaho. Canton checked his collection of wanted posters and, sure enough, he found Barkley among the photos. Idaho offered a reward of $2,500.

In the evening, shortly after this discovery, Canton took his supper with the boat captain, ship's clerk, and the clerk's wife. He spoke to them openly about Barkley's status as a wanted criminal. Canton told the dinner group that he planned to slap Barkley in irons as soon as the ice went out. Once they made Canada he planned to deliver the fugitive to the Mounties and collect the reward money. During the conversation the clerk's wife listened intently. Occasionally, she asked for details. Canton thought it somewhat odd that she expressed such curiosity in his shop talk, but he shrugged it off.

A few nights later at dusk, Canton boarded the steamer and opened the cabin door. At that instant a man hidden in the brush nearby fired a shot. The hot lead screamed by his ear to lodge with a sickening thud in the door. It had missed its target by mere inches. Canton reacted as though he had been shot. The crash of the bullet into the wood sent up splinters which lodged in his face. He quickly realized that his wound was minor as he jumped through the door into the room.

Canton wiped the blood from his face, grabbed his rifle, took a deep breath, and sprinted down the gangplank and into the brush to look for footprints. He soon found some and followed them in the snow to Barkley's cabin. He ignored his impulse to kill Barkley on the spot. Canton wanted the reward, but it would be much easier to deliver a live body than a dead one. He decided to wait until the ice went out to arrest Barkley. Canton kept an eye on him and had his deputies assist in the twenty-four-hour watch.

The surveillance revealed that the clerk's wife was having an affair with the outlaw. This shocked Canton, who wrote later that the discovery convinced him that he knew virtually nothing about women. He decided to arrest Barkley immediately, since the outlaw knew about his plans.

As Canton made his move, the ice in the river began to move as well. Within a matter of minutes the air was thick with the noise of cracking ice. Canton likened it to the sound of thousands of tons of dynamite going off. Pieces of ice ten feet thick and the size of an acre of land suddenly got pushed up out of the river and then slammed down. The impact flattened and uprooted trees on the riverbanks. Large icebergs flowed down the river and spun in the water like pinwheels.

The camp residents initially reacted calmly to the spectacle. They believed that the camp was on high ground and thus safe. In a moment they realized their folly. Large chunks of ice came crashing into the camp, instantly flooding it to a depth of five feet of water. The current-driven ice ripped cabins apart as if they were built of twigs. The men and women of the camp suddenly found themselves fighting for their lives in deathly cold water. Many of them climbed trees or to the rooftops of cabins.

Canton and some of the men aboard the steamboats struggled to protect the vessels as best they could. The captain pressed all of the skiffs and lifeboats into service. Those who fared well in the initial blast of ice did what they could to help those caught by the raging water and ice.

Suddenly, Canton noticed that the clerk and his wife were on the roof of a cabin close by the steamer. They called for help as the rushing water lapped midway up to the roof. To get to them, someone would need to row out into the main channel of the Yukon. It was a suicide mission. The sight was too much to bear for the men who could do nothing to save them.

When it seemed all hope was lost, Barkley and some of his gang came up along the side of the steamer, floating on logs. They asked permission to take out the rowboat to lend some assistance. The captain gave them a boat and a long pole to fight off the ice. Out they went into the whirlpool of ice and raging waters. Canton thought that they were heading for certain death. He watched in awe at the audacity and bravery they displayed. The river tossed the boat violently. Several times it looked as though it would capsize.

Somehow, Barkley and his men rowed out through the raging waters of the main current into a back eddy that gave them access to the cabin. The clerk and his wife quickly slid into the boat. As it pushed off, they looked back at the cabin and watched as it crumbled into the swift main current of the Yukon. Barkley then rowed the boat toward higher ground to wait out the flood.

Canton exhaled a breath of relief. It had been, he wrote later, the "most splendid exhibition of nerve that I ever witnessed. I could not help but feel that it was a great pity that such men should have chosen the crooked trail of crime instead of being real men among men." Only one other man in the camp besides Canton knew what had inspired Barkley to perform this heroic act. The two lawmen told no one else.

As the river settled down, the camp took stock. Everyone dried themselves and their clothes, salvaged what they could from the damage, and waited for the river to become navigable. Barkley still had the lifeboat, so Canton kept an eagle eye on him. In the evening, he saw Barkley and a woman in the boat heading for a cabin that had not been destroyed.

Canton followed them and overheard the woman beg Barkley not to make her leave her husband. Barkley told her that he had no choice because she was the only woman he had ever loved. He protested his innocence of any crimes. She had to go with him down to St. Michael, return to the States, and marry him. She finally relented and promised to go with him. Barkley sent her to pack and asked her to be ready to leave in twenty minutes.

Barkley then prepared to steal the lifeboat and supplies for the journey to St. Michael. While he was thus engaged, Canton snuck up behind him with his revolver drawn and tapped him on the shoulder. He ordered Barkley to put his hands up and turn around. After he disarmed Barkley, Canton rattled off a list of reasons why he should put a bullet through him right then and there, beginning with the three murders in Idaho; the reward money on his head; Barkley's attempt to murder him; and Barkley's plan to bring a good woman to ruin.

The lawman then gave Barkley some options: Canton could shoot him now and collect the reward, or slap him in irons and see him tried in Idaho. But Canton told him that he would do neither—a comment that must have confused the outlaw. No, Canton said, he had been stirred by Barkley's heroic rescue of the clerk and his wife. It meant, Canton believed, that there was still a spark of good in the murderous thief. Canton planned to turn Barkley loose and give him one last chance to "make good."

The memory of Joe Horner, the repentant old outlaw, moved Canton at that moment. Everyone deserved another chance, even murderers like Horner. With that thought, Canton—or was it the repentant Horner?—told Barkley to get in the lifeboat and toss out his firearms along with one of the oars. He did not want Barkley to try to pull upstream against the current and come after him. Then he shoved Barkley off and watched him drift down the Yukon.

As he floated downstream in the swift current, Barkley swore an oath that if he ever got the chance, he would kill Canton. Barkley never got that opportunity. He floated down the Yukon and into obscurity, while Canton traveled to Circle to take his post.

George O'Brien

There was no doubt about it: Leo Reid had gold fever. News of the strikes in the Yukon Territory of Canada's Far Northern Wilderness circulated for more than a year through the bars, brothels, and hotels of San Francisco in the late 1890s. Reid knew that the early stampeders had already filed claims to all the best locations. Still, he recognized that there was yet money to be made in the Klondike. All of those men who rushed to the gold streams had money to spend, even if it was borrowed. Reid planned to open up a gambling house in Dawson. It would be the next best thing to a paying stake, and not half the hard work required by a claim. The entrepreneur possessed some capital to invest. San Francisco had grown tiresome, and he itched for excitement.

Reid steamed up the Inside passage, offloaded in Skagway, bought the best outfit he could in that bustling gateway to the Klondike, and headed out to cover the 600 miles to Dawson as fast as he could. It was a long journey for one impatient to make a new start and who dreamed of untold riches. Only green-horns drove their dogs too hard, though. What good would it do to maintain an overly fast pace only to lose dogs on the way and possibly strand yourself on the trail? No, Reid remained patient and took his time. In San Francisco he heard many stories about the mistakes made by newcomers. He resolved not to make any. Caution and prudence remained his watchwords. He was quietly confident in his abilities, believing it was the mark of a real man to know one's limits. Besides, he had not set out to prove his manhood or to impress strangers. His goal was to get rich, not get killed.

Reid's days on the trail and over the pass pushed his endurance and often left him exhausted, but they remained uneventful and he enjoyed the challenge. Life on the trail, the crisp, cool air, and the exertion invigorated one's spirit. Meeting the physical challenges of nature satisfied Western outdoorsmen in ways that city folk back east did not often understand.

Before arriving in Dawson, Reid stopped at a little camp occupied by George O'Brien. O'Brien welcomed him, treated Reid well, and told him to stay and rest his dogs for as long as he wanted. After weeks of hard work with his dog team on the trail, Reid welcomed the friendly hospitality. He enjoyed the company of O'Brien, and tried to learn what he could from him about life in the Klondike. He never suspected that O'Brien had recently murdered two men traveling from Dawson to Skagway.

After a few days of good rest, Reid and his dogs were ready to make the final leg of the long journey. As he said his farewells, O'Brien asked him if he would swap some food for one of his dogs. Reid recognized the value of a good dog in those parts, and agreed to trade some bacon and flour. He attached the dog to his team and said good-bye to O'Brien.

Reid finally made it into Dawson and happily found a camp to stake out his dogs and cache his gear and supplies on the edge of town. He got cleaned up as best he could under the circumstances and then headed toward Main Street to see the town, get a good meal, and have a drink.

As he surveyed his surroundings Reid saw Al Hoyle, an old friend from San Francisco. Reid was darn happy to see a familiar face, and greeted his old pal with a wide smile on his face and a hard slap on the back. The two chatted for a while to get caught up and to spin some yarns about the old times in San Francisco. The talk eventually shifted to more contemporary events, and the town of Dawson. Hoyle told Reid that the town was burning up with news of a robbery and murder on the trail from Skagway that Reid had just traveled. He wanted to know if his old friend had heard or seen anything along the trail.

This question piqued Reid's curiosity. He reported that nothing extraordinary had happened during his journey from Skagway. Did Hoyle know any of the details? Who was killed? How much was taken? Where did it happen? Did the Mounties have any suspects? Hoyle told Reid that the holdup had taken

A sled dog team and their admirers stand on a snow-covered Skagway street, c.a. 1898. *Alaska State Library, William R. Norton Photographs, P266-096.*

place about a day or two out of Dawson. The Mounties suspected a man called George O'Brien, Hoyle reported.

Reid blanched at this last comment. He could not believe it! O'Brien had been so cordial and friendly to him in camp. Could there be more than one man called O'Brien? He told Hoyle of his encounter at O'Brien's camp, and that he had traded some food for one of the suspect's dogs. It was a distinctive-looking animal.

Hoyle's jaw dropped at the news that Reid had just been in O'Brien's camp. He told Reid to take him to the dog immediately. The two walked down the boardwalk past the saloons and eating establishments to the edge of Dawson, where Reid had left his dogs and gear. As they walked into the little camp where the dogs rested on fresh straw, the animals hardly stirred. With full stomachs and comfortable beds, they barely noticed the arrival of the two men. After 600 miles on the trail, they were happy to have this luxury, and demonstrated their contentment with a few lazy glances in their direction and a few exaggerated yawns.

Reid showed Hoyle the dog he had gotten from O'Brien. It only took a momentary glance for Hoyle to confirm that the animal had once belonged to the murder suspect. There was no doubt about it. O'Brien had purchased the dog in Skagway some time ago. Everyone knew the animal because of its unusual markings. That explained some of the stares Reid had received from men on the boardwalk when he had first arrived in town. The townsmen seemed obsessed with the crime and the manhunt. They talked of almost nothing else. In fact, the news of the newcomer, who had traveled with O'Brien's dog, rapidly spread through the boomtown.

Hoyle urged Reid to get rid of the dog quickly. If the authorities found out that he had stayed at O'Brien's camp, they would put him in jail and hold him as a material witness. Reid might be laid up for a year or more depending on how long it took to capture O'Brien and try him. The thought of that made Reid a little queasy. He did not make the long and arduous journey to Dawson to rot in a jail cell simply for conversing (unknowingly) with a criminal.

Reid immediately turned the dog loose, but the dog had ideas of his own. The animal followed Reid back into town. Reid then tried to give it away, but everyone knew whose dog it had been, and no one showed any interest in owning him. Finally, Reid took the dog to the other side of the town in the middle of the night, tied up the animal, and left him there. The poor, unwanted beast whimpered as Reid walked away.

Meanwhile, the police heard rumors that witnesses had spotted O'Brien in town. The Mounties now combed the trail leading to Dawson, and the city itself block by block, to find the murder suspect. They found the dog and used him in their search. As they interviewed the residents of Dawson, they watched the dog to see if he recognized anyone. Perhaps the animal might help uncover O'Brien or his gang members. Reid laid low during this dragnet; he knew that the dog would recognize him.

Mounties scoured the trail from Dawson to Skagway as well. News soon reached Dawson that the Mounties had got their man! They brought him into Dawson and lodged him in the jail to await trial and execution.

Information about the investigation leaked from the jail and into the community. O'Brien was like many other men who had traveled to the gold fields to get rich quick. They held unrealistic expectations that the gold lay atop the gravel in the streams, just waiting to be harvested. Such stories germinated in excited people, who spread the stories and rumors that they had heard from those who *had* struck a mother lode, or from someone who claimed to know someone who did.

These stories often represented the imaginings or idealizations of what the people who told the stories wanted to believe. They revealed a deep-seated desire for easy wealth; in a word, it was greed. There were plenty of people in North America, Europe, and elsewhere in the world who dreamed of easy wealth. So, when such stories were spread through the media and word of mouth, many hopeful people willed themselves to believe.

During the era of the Klondike strike at the turn of the twentieth century, many Americans faced hardship and tumultuous change. America was in transition, moving from a rural and agrarian-based economy to an urban and industrial one. The country had recently experienced a devastating economic depression, the Panic of 1893. In addition, large monopolies had emerged due to an unprecedented increase in corporate mergers. The growing power of corporate monopolies undermined the strength of unions. Hundreds of thousands of immigrants crowded into the country, seeking fortune and security. This infusion of cheap labor further weakened the power of the working class. Men in the West moved from community to community in search of work that would pay more than subsistence wages. By this time, most of the mining had been taken over by larger, highly capitalized companies. The options for prospectors and independent miners were drying up as competition for laborers in the corporate mines increased. Violent encounters arose between capital and labor, and among different ethnic groups competing for work.

News of the Klondike strike and others elsewhere always offered hope to the working men that they might be able to break out of the wage slavery that they found themselves in. All they needed was a grubstake, some pluck, and naturally, some luck. Of course, the gritty reality of these gold rushes was that many heeded the news of the strike, but only a few could realistically expect to make even a modest amount of money. Whenever expectations are high, but only a few actually realize that level of success, there are predictable side effects: disappointment, depression, resignation, anger, and resentment.

So, take a large number of angry and resentful men in their twenties and thirties. Place them hundreds or even thousands of miles away from home in a remote location. Add alcohol, subtract institutions of behavioral control such as religion, marriage, and law, and you have a recipe for trouble and violence. Although the Canadian side of the border was typically much more orderly than the U.S. side, there was still a relative deficiency of institutions that helped keep order in society. The throngs of American prospectors that crossed into Canada had their own notions about freedom and liberty as well.

George O'Brien had come to the Far North like many other prospectors, hoping to get rich quick. He soon learned the reality of conditions in the Dawson area. Unlike most stampeders, however, he was a brutally cold and calculating man. When it became clear that the only ones getting rich were a lucky few with good claims, and the merchants and companies that serviced the miners, he came to a dark conclusion. The one sure way to get rich in the Klondike was to steal the fruits of some-one else's labor. O'Brien put together a plan and organized a gang to implement it.

The O'Brien gang set up camp 200 miles outside of Daw-son. Just off the trail and strategically located next to a body of water that remained unfrozen all winter, it attracted the atten-tion of travelers. There the gang planned to lay in wait for those few who had successfully accumulated a vast amount of wealth in the gold streams. To catch a steamship back to the States required making the 600-mile overland journey to Skagway first, and the trail passed right through the O'Brien trap.

The key to the gang's plan lay in their ability to get informa-tion about men on the trail from Dawson. They did not want to waste their time and luck on poor men. O'Brien sent one gang member back into town on the dogsled with the team to keep an eye out for big talkers and bigshots who boasted of their good fortune. When he found a likely target, O'Brien instructed him, he would head out on the trail to give the gang a warning. The gang would then set up an ambush for the unsuspecting victims.

No one knows for sure how many men were hijacked in this manner. O'Brien's gang actively worked this scheme for several months before Reid came up the trail. Some suggested that as many as seventy-five men might have been robbed and murdered, their bodies thrown into the Yukon River never to be seen again. While this number seems absurdly high, there were many potential victims of this holdup scheme. Numerous people seemed to have disappeared without a trace during this time period. How many were victims of foul play will never be known. Once people left Dawson to return to their places of origin or cities on the West Coast, no one in Dawson expected to hear from them again. That was the brilliance of O'Brien's plan—or so he thought, anyway.

Just before Reid arrived in O'Brien's camp from Skagway, a party of prospectors carrying $80,000 in gold that they had acquired in the Klondike began to make the trek from Dawson to Skagway. The O'Brien gang received word from their spy that three men with a huge sum of money were on their way. The gang prepared to spring the trap. The party consisted of three men who owned one of the best-producing claims in the Klondike gold fields. When they got into the camp, O'Brien's gang caught them completely by surprise. Before they knew what had hit them, they found themselves staring down the barrels of the O'Brien gang's guns.

These prospectors had been around for a while. When O'Brien commanded them to drop their holstered guns and reach for the sky, they knew that either way, they were likely to be shot and killed. So in response to O'Brien's instructions, they responded in unison. They threw down all right, but not in the expected compliant manner. Each of them boldly went for their sidearms and drew them in self-defense.

The fight was on. Lead filled the air, and the acrid odor of spent gunpowder wafted through the camp. In a matter of seconds the game appeared to be up and the deed was done. Two of the courageous prospectors lay dying. The third, overwhelmed by the odds, ran off in a valiant effort to make a good escape.

O'Brien did not expect or plan for this development. It was a bad situation for the gang. The prospector not only possessed a good and relatively fresh dog team, but the sled also contained all of the money the gang had planned to steal. Not only did the gang watch their huge payday sliding down the trail on the fast-moving sled, but they also confronted the certainty that the lone survivor would immediately report the murders to the police when he reached Skagway. This fact panicked the gang. If their victims had been forced to use the only trail linking Dawson to the shipping lanes, they faced the same reality. The only way out was to go through Dawson and down the long Yukon River, or the shorter route down to Skagway. Either way, the gang would soon face a manhunt for them.

O'Brien's gang had no choice but to make pursuit. One problem remained, however, and that was a lack of dogs. All they had in the camp on this day was a horse and sleigh. It made for very comfortable travel compared to a dogsled, but it was much slower on account of the weight of the animal and the deepness of the snow in the Yukon Territory at that time of year. The horse kept breaking through the crust of the hard-packed trail. The dogs traveled quite efficiently in comparison, without breaking through the snow.

Cursing as he went, O'Brien figured out pretty quick that he was engaged in a futile effort. After a few miles he gave up and turned back to camp. He began to work out a plan to take the loot accumulated by the gang and make a getaway before the authorities were on to them. As soon as the surviving prospector made Skagway, the authorities would come looking for O'Brien and his gang. There was little time to lose, and O'Brien quickly put together an escape plan.

O'Brien knew that the White Mountain Railroad was currently building the White Pass line from Skagway to Dawson. The company had cut a trail and workers had graded the road in preparation for the ties and rails to be laid soon. O'Brien took that new route on foot. But five Northwest Mounted Police caught up with him on a trestle that was under construction. When they took him into custody, the Mounties asked O'Brien what had happened to his partner. He told them that his partner had taken his horse and that he expected to meet the man on the other side of the trestle. Although they waited for some time and did some looking, the Mounties found no trace of a horse and rider in the area. His partner never surfaced anywhere as far as the authorities could discover. Given the violent reputation of O'Brien, the Mounties concluded that he had murdered his partner and taken all of the money for himself.

Just before O'Brien's spy in Dawson heard the news of his boss's capture, he had been in Monte Carlo and made $2,000 gambling that night. He never got the chance to use his winnings. Although he fled town immediately upon learning that the authorities held O'Brien, he was eventually captured in Skagway while waiting to catch a steamer to Seattle.

At his trial, and again just before his execution by hanging, authorities attempted to get O'Brien to name his missing partner and all of his victims. Officials tried to appeal to his better side by asking him to think about the victims' loved ones, who had no idea what had become of their men. O'Brien apparently no longer cared about humanity, for he refused to cooperate. He coldly told his executioners that he did not know how many men he had killed, did not know their names, and did not care about them or their families.

Reid watched the trial proceedings. It was a strange experience for him to witness. There was the cordial man of the camp that he had stayed with just before his arrival in Dawson. He had enjoyed O'Brien's hospitality and conversation for several days. He had traded some of his food for O'Brien's dog. He never would have conceived that this man was a brutal and heartless murderer. What a close call; what luck, he must have thought to himself as he sat through the proceedings. The court did not call Reid to the stand as a witness. But then, only O'Brien, Reid, and his friend Hoyle knew anything about Reid's encounter with a murderer. Reid thought it remarkable how the cold and stoic O'Brien just sat there in his chair when the jury rendered the verdict and the judge sentenced him to death by hanging. O'Brien did not flinch; he showed no emotion, and in fact, seemed to not care at all. Later, when the condemned man walked up to the scaffold, his face presented the same indifferent demeanor.

He said no last words, but preferred instead to take the secrets of his grim career to his grave. When he got to the top platform of the scaffold, he looked blankly beyond the few spectators. An executioner placed a hood over his head. Down below, three taut cords ran up through the scaffolding. One of these cords was attached to the trapdoor on which O'Brien stood waiting for oblivion. It was not clear which cord was attached to the lever that held the trapdoor closed. Jailers brought out three shackled inmates serving life sentences. They stood behind a screen to which the cords had been stretched. Each man was assigned a cord to cut that would potentially release the trap and send O'Brien plunging toward the cold concrete floor. None of these convicts would ever know if their cord was the one keeping O'Brien alive in his last moments on earth. The order to pull the cords came. O'Brien came crashing down through the trapdoor. His body hung in death throes. Then, officials declared O'Brien dead. They buried his remains near Dawson in a grave with no marker.

The Sheep Camp Vigilantes of Chilkoot Pass

The crack of the lash echoed through the camp, followed a split second later by a singular cry of pain and a murmur of approval from the crowd of spectators. Edward Hansen, a young Swedish immigrant, had borne the first few stripes from the whip with stoicism. Stripped to the waist and tied to a stump, this captive of vigilante miners could no longer suffer the violations of the whip without involuntary protestations.

Hansen must have pondered his fate in the seconds between the blows his increasingly purple back endured. There he was, surrounded by hundreds of angry miners, his four flannel shirts lying in the snow. The mercury at noon rose only to 10 degrees below zero. The bone-chilling cold intensified the pain and damage being inflicted to his back. Not even a quarter of the way through his sentence of fifty lashes, he begged to be hanged rather than suffering this excruciating flogging.

A few of the softer-hearted men in the crowd, unable to bear Hansen's pathetic cries and whimpering, began to speak out on his behalf, asking for mercy. The hard-core men of the camp drowned them out with their demands for satisfaction. A crime had been committed against all miners heading for the Klondike gold fields; justice demanded full implementation of the sentence. In their view, Hansen's suffering represented a deterrent to all other would-be thieves. This was frontier justice!

One hundred yards away, William Wellington, Hansen's alleged partner in crime, lay dead in the blood-soaked snow. His face was gone, destroyed by the bullet that he himself had sent into his brains moments after his attempt to run away from the vigilance committee "court." He knew he could not escape its vengeance, so he went out on his own terms. Ironically, his suicide simultaneously spared Hansen from the hangman's noose, but consigned him to a fate that he now felt was worse than swinging by the neck from a tree.

The miners' court wanted their pound of flesh, and they meant to get it now from Hansen. By the look on his face and the condition of the tattered flesh on his back, they were getting it. Many of the miners at Sheep Camp on the trail to Chilkoot Pass, and those on a rival trail over White Pass, had lost their cached supplies to thieves such as Wellington and Hansen. The miners used their frontier code of justice to send a message to all thieves on the trails to the gold fields.

According to contemporary observers, it appeared to work. Cache-pillaging incidents seemed to decrease significantly after the Sheep Camp vigilante movement took action. Even Alaska Territorial governor John Brady, although he did not condone such vigilante actions, noted the positive impact this incident had on law and order on the Klondike trails. Other constituted authorities, however, demanded the names of the leaders who had organized the camp meeting, run the proceedings, and meted out the punishment. The miners responded to the demand by daring the authorities to come and get them, if they were man enough. They apparently were not, and never did go after the vigilante leaders.

At the height of the Klondike gold rush, men from across the world clamored to get at the diggings to stake a claim before the gold was gone. Many of these men, and a few women, went with the intent to prey upon the hardworking majority. They sought by hook, crook, or deceit to relieve these men of their money. Still others put in with this human current to see where it would take them on their entrepreneurial voyage to the northern diggings. They too wanted to get rich on the hard labors of the men digging in the sand and gravel for placer gold. But they followed a path recognized as legal: high markups on items they sold to the prospectors!

These entrepreneurs understood that the odds of striking the mother lode, despite the hype and hullabaloo, were long. The smart money was invested in marketing the gear, clothing, and food to the stampeders. It was not as romantic or manly to sell dry goods. These merchants, save a few of the more colorful men and women or highly capitalized ventures that plied their wares on the northern frontier, have not been celebrated like the miners and prostitutes for their work in pioneering the North.

It has always been the miners, the so-called rugged individualists, who have been portrayed in the frontier myth as the leading force that developed an Alaskan economy and frontier society. Well, there are myths and then there are more realistic historical assessments of the Last Frontier's development. Amateur historians and antiquarians have tended to focus on the sourdoughs, but prospectors remained dependent on the merchants and bankers for capital and supplies that grubstaked their manly—and more often, vain—efforts to strike it rich. The miners provided the labor, but the merchants and capitalists funded, organized, and made possible the efforts of miners who, though they were rugged, were hardly independent.

It was difficult to keep track of the throngs of men and women who rushed to the Klondike diggings. Most of them caught a steamer up from Seattle or San Francisco through the Inside Passage and landed at Dyea or Skagway. They were required by the Canadian government to bring with them one ton of supplies to ensure that they were properly equipped for the hardships they might face in the Yukon Territory. During the height of the rush of 1898, thousands of men made their way over the beaches at Dyea and Skagway, the first stage of their effort to get to the Klondike gold fields. They unloaded their gear on the beaches and began to move their supplies in stages up the trails. It took numerous trips up and down the trails from the beaches to the passes. As a result, there were perhaps hundreds of caches scattered along the trails.

Men who could afford the services of Tlingit Indians paid them to do the bulk of the heavy hauling work. The Tlingits were a large and powerful cultural group who occupied much of the Northwest Coast of Alaska, including the Chilkoot and White Pass areas. They had lived in these ancestral lands for centuries before the arrival of the first Russian fur traders in the mid-eighteenth century. Tlingits used the mountain passes to access the Interior trade networks developed hundreds of years earlier. For about a century during the Russian-American era, the Tlingits played off one power against another and prospered. They were armed and well versed in the arts of warfare. Their resistance to the Russians played an important role in the latter's eventual decision to sell Alaska to the United States in 1867.

The Tlingits, then, were not a passive or conquered people when the Americans began to arrive in Alaska in the late nineteenth century. They jealously guarded access to their homeland. When Americans began to go up the trails into the Klondike in the 1880s, they were obliged to pay a toll for the privilege of using Tlingit trails. Eventually, the might of the American military was brought to bear against the Tlingits. This show of force convinced the Indians to concede their trails to the newcomers.

The trails used by the stampeders of '98 had been well used by Tlingit traders over the past centuries. The Tlingits may have been forced to allow Europeans to use their trails without tolls, but they found other ways to make the stampeders pay. The Tlingits possessed legendary strength, and soon they were in high demand as packers. This strength enabled many to make good profits from their labors, moving supplies across the pass to the Canadian side. The average American packer could carry about 45 pounds on his back, but most Tlingit packers could carry an amazing 100-pound pack. One legendary Tlingit individual stood out from the rest when he carried a 350-pound barrel over the pass.

In addition to their physical strength, the Tlingits also knew how to survive in the coastal mountains. They were especially adept at understanding snow conditions along the pass. During the Easter season in 1898, warming weather and new snow combined to make conditions on the ascent up the Chilkoot Pass extremely dangerous. None of the Tlingit packers would take money, regardless of the amount offered, to pack supplies during this time. They knew that such conditions created the danger of avalanche. The snow had been falling for several days, and rendered the pass impregnable until the sun finally returned.

A view of the Chilkoot Trail winding through Sheep Camp near timberline and Chilkoot Pass, c.a. 1897. *Alaska State Library, Charles Horton Metcalfe Photograph Collection, P34-003.*

The return of the sun and warmer temperatures had many stampeders chomping at the bit to get moving to the gold fields. The Tlingits warned the stampeders, but many did not listen. These men paid dearly for their stopped-up ears. On April 3, 1898, Easter Sunday, at least sixty stampeders were killed in an avalanche that came thundering down 2,500 feet onto the trail from steep hillsides on both sides of the trail. The avalanche covered ten acres with thirty feet of hard-packed, cement-like snow. Within a few minutes, hundreds of men came up from Sheep Camp to try to help the entombed survivors. Many of those buried alive could be heard conversing with others in the snow. Others spoke futilely to those who tried to rescue them.

One man was said to be heard praying and then cursing and then praying again. Rescuers only saved a few men.

Most stampeders crossing Chilkoot and White passes in 1898 were not in a position to pay Tlingits to pack their supplies over the mountains. They moved their supplies one backload at a time up the trail. Sheep Camp was 13 miles up the trail from Dyea and 4 miles away from Chilkoot Pass. It became a sprawling tent city during the halcyon days of the rush. As many as 1,500 men at a time lived in tents, shanties, and shacks along a wooded valley. It was, for a time, a key staging point for hundreds of men working up a sweat in the Southeast Alaska winter. From there, the supplies needed to be moved to the base of the pass in preparation for the most arduous part of the journey, packing the supplies up and over the famed Chilkoot Pass. Then it was down the other side of the mountains and another 500 miles on the Yukon River to the gold fields of the Yukon Territory in Canada.

William Wellington and his partner in crime, Edward Hansen, were among the nameless and faceless throng in 1898, until the lure of the unguarded caches overpowered them and they succumbed. No one can say for sure when Wellington and Hansen arrived in Skagway. Most people in the tent village were transient, leaving as soon as possible to move their gear and supplies up the trail to White Pass. During early February, though, the two men began plotting to take advantage of the hundreds of cached goods along the trail from the beach to White Pass.

Few stampeders worked alone; those that did were at a disadvantage. They did not have support and companionship during the hard or high times. More important, there was no one to watch their back. They were on their own in a rough-and-tumble environment. It was just this sort of person that the two would-be cache robbers were looking for. Wellington and Hansen sought certain advantages in numbers. Their target would have to leave his gear unguarded and trust in the miners' code of honor to protect his property from thieves. The two crooked men did not adhere to the code. And, if the target happened upon the thieves in their act of crime, they could easily overpower him.

Wellington and Hansen made their move in early February. The snow was hard packed and a little sparse the day they found the unguarded cache of the lone prospector. They were in luck because their victim had left his sled there as well, making their crime and escape that much easier. They loaded up his entire outfit and made their way back down the trail from Skagway to White Pass. They were planning to get lost in the chaotic scene of the Skagway beach, with its mobs of stampeders trying to quickly unload their gear in preparation to move it over the pass.

When they got to Skagway, they were not disappointed. Men were scrambling all over the lawless town. Dogs were barking, and supplies were stacked in disorderly piles in every conceivable location. The scene was pure bedlam. It appeared that the entire town of roughly 8,000 was out on the beach. The two men looked at each other with a grin as they pulled into Skagway. They could taste the alcohol already; and there isn't anything much sweeter than a drink bought with someone else's money. But, for now, the two resisted the urge to get smashed. Their illicit work remained incomplete.

They placed the supplies into a rowboat, pushed off from the beach, and pulled hard on the oars as they made for nearby Dyea, the tent town competing with Skagway to be the gateway to the Klondike. The plan seemed foolproof to the two men. Their victim would never think to track them down to Dyea. He might look for them in Skagway, but by then his gear and supplies would have been sold bit by bit to numerous unwary prospectors.

At the time, the two scoundrels did not realize that a man had followed them. None of the historical accounts provide the name of Wellington and Hansen's victim. The nameless one, however, became an unrelenting opponent of the thieves. He faithfully pursued them to recover his property and to get frontier justice. When Wellington and Hansen made Dyea in good time, he was close behind them. There they joined the chaos of that community and unloaded their gear from the rowboat and carefully stacked it back on the sled. They wasted little time getting on the trail to Chilkoot Pass.

Although it was difficult to pass by the saloons and ignore the revelry as they moved down the main street, the two outlaws had dishonest work to attend to before they could take their rest. Onward up the trail they pulled until they made Sheep Camp. Here, they would offer their stolen wares for sale in what they thought was complete safety from discovery.

Their relentless pursuer caught up with them at Sheep Camp. Before reaching this location the angry victim had always hung back, cautious to not get too close until the right time presented itself. Now that the thieves had stopped to set up their shop in a crowded camp, he made his move. Sheep Camp was a bustling little tent city in its own right. It was the

161

last place on the trail to find good water and wood for camp before the trail to the summit began. A few entrepreneurs had built cabins and roadhouses to skim away the profits of the men going to and from the diggings. The favored watering hole was housed in a circus big top–style tent and naturally went by the name of the Big Tent Saloon.

While the thieves began to sell the stolen goods, their pursuer moseyed around the camp to get a feel for the tenor of the residents. He needed allies in this lawless location, for he could not handle the two men alone. Moreover, the miners might not tolerate him simply taking the law into his own hands. The miners lived by an unwritten code that helped keep peace and order, such as it was, on the trails and in the gold fields. The victim asked around the camp if anyone had had anything stolen from their caches lately. He soon found an undercurrent of rage beneath the surface calm of the camp.

Many men had had their caches looted of some or all their contents. They had all suffered the injustice and indignity in more or less silence. It would be unmanly to allow their rage at a personal misfortune to tarnish their reputations as rugged individuals capable of weathering any storm. But all men have their boiling point, and sometimes it takes very little to reach it. The persistent victim of the crime knew that he had found allies, so he confidently made his next move.

He revealed his plight to a few of the permanent camp residents and pointed out the identity of the men in question. The Sheep Camp residents quickly organized a meeting of the camp's most influential men. They concluded that it was time to make an example of the two thieves; the crime spree had gone on long enough, and it was time to bring it to a close.

They dispatched some men to capture the suspects. These men quickly and easily accomplished the task. Others posted and passed out handbills around the camp to notify residents of a meeting to take place on February 15 at the Big Tent Saloon. This meeting of a miners' court would, the notices stated, deal with two known thieves. The sourdoughs recognized the meaning of this meeting: An unofficial trial would be held, placing the fate of the two thieves in the collective hands of the camp.

As the appointed hour approached, miners gathered in the saloon under the light of oil lamps and candles. It was quite a scene, this informal gathering of men from across the globe. The Big Tent Saloon had been emptied of most of its contents to make room for the large crowd. The miners of the camp elected a chairman to act as a judge over the proceedings, and a committee of men to assist and advise him. This "court" was seated on a rough-hewn board supported at both ends by wooden crates. A plain slab of wood, placed in the middle of the tent, served as a table. A wooden box provided a seat for each of the accused men, who would be interviewed individually by the court. The entire camp, or at least those who could sit in the six or seven rows of seats surrounding the court on all sides, would act as a jury.

Many colorful characters in the camp came to the event for a variety of reasons. Some were motivated by the opportunity for a break in the boring routine, while others came for the spectacle. Many had grievances with thieves and sought a cathartic resolution to their frustrations, and, of course, many attended to satisfy a taste for blood sport. No doubt about it—this little scene of frontier justice provided the best entertainment for hundreds if not thousands of miles around. It also represented an exercise in plain-folk democracy. Some believed that such proceedings held more legitimacy than courts conducted by constituted authorities Outside, back in the States.

The two accused men took turns separately in front of the frontier camp tribunal. They had been held in custody apart from each other and interrogated individually. When they presented their respective stories to the judge and jury, they clearly did not match. The court brought them both back into the tent for a subsequent grilling in the interrogation chair. This process was repeated several times until their fabricated stories unraveled like a cheap cotton shirt on a hardworking miner.

Each defendant stared at his filthy boots and watched as his feet fidgeted on the dirt floor of the Big Tent. Aside from their possession of stolen goods, the testimony of their accuser, and the problems with their changing and mismatched accounts of the events, the main evidence that implicated Wellington and Hansen was the name on the frozen runner of the sled that the two men had stolen. It matched that of the plaintiff who had doggedly pursued them from the White Pass trail to Skagway, by boat to Dyea, up the Chilkoot Trail, and, finally, to Sheep Camp.

The jury wasted little time in their deliberations and quickly reached a decision. The lead jurist told the judge that the jury had found both defendants guilty as charged. At that instant, Wellington leaped up from his seat on the wood box, pulled out a pistol and a blade that he had secreted on his person, slashed the tent canvas, and ran into the cold, wet Southeast Alaskan night. Initially stunned by this sudden action, the miners in the Big Tent recovered quickly from this daring escape attempt. Miners moved to the torn tent wall and to the main entrance to give chase.

The first man through the new exit sliced in the canvas wall paid for his quick reflexes. Wellington hit him with a bullet fired wildly over his shoulder as he headed as fast as he could away from the tent and into the darkness. The sound of the wounded man's cries in response to his volley at the candlelit tent hole must have given Wellington an added surge of adrenaline and incentive to make good his escape. He had now added attempted murder to his list of crimes, for which the miners had attempted to extract frontier justice.

Back at the Big Tent, the anger of the miners boiled over. Many cried out for volunteers to go after Wellington and to shoot him. One man screamed for someone to get a dog team; Wellington would not be able to leave the trail, he noted, because of the drifted snow. Surely a dog team would catch up to him in short order. Just as the miners had begun to sort out the chaos and the miners' committee had organized an orderly pursuit, another shot rang out. The men paused, looked at each other, and then speculated on the meaning of the second shot.

Wellington had made good time down the trail through Sheep Camp, but several miners quickly gained on him. The fugitive had not made it out of the camp when Addison Mizner, who later in the 1920s emerged as one of the most colorful figures in the real estate boom in Florida, got near striking distance. In the darkness, no one could make out exactly what was happening. There was the noise of men running. Men's lungs gasped for and expelled bursts of air that hung fog-like in the air. In the moonlight, macabre shadows seemed to mimic a death dance on the snow as Mizner closed in on Wellington.

Suddenly, as Mizner reached out to tackle his quarry, another shot rang out. The two men crashed into a tent and were soon covered in blood. Seconds later, the other miners in pursuit caught up to the two downed men. They involuntarily paused for a moment when they saw the blood. Then they regained their composure and reached down to lift Wellington off of Mizner, not knowing who had been hit. Wellington's limp body remained motionless as they lifted him and rolled him over onto the snow. His face was no longer recognizable. Mizner, stunned by the explosion of Wellington's gun and covered in his blood, did not seem to know what had happened, or if he had been hit. The Mizner brothers—Edgar, William, and Wilson—breathed a sigh of relief when they discovered that their brother Addison had not been shot. Everyone slapped each other on the back, shared a nervous laugh, and headed back to the Big Tent Saloon with news of the resolution of Wellington's case.

Back at the saloon, in the flickering light, hushed men waited expectantly for news regarding the second gunshot that they had heard. Within moments a miner ran up to the Big Tent Saloon, stuck his head through the entryway, and said, "It's all right, boys; Wellington has shot himself and is lying in the trail now." Instantly the miners gave out a collective hurrah in the tent and then ran outside and down the trail to get a look at Wellington's remains where they lay in the snow, about 100 yards away. They also wanted to convince themselves that he was actually dead by his own hand.

A few miners with kerosene lanterns held them over the body to reveal a gruesome visage. Just before Mizner had tackled him, Wellington had placed the muzzle of his .45 caliber revolver to his forehead. Preferring to choose his own destiny rather than leave his fate up to the miners' court, Wellington pulled the trigger. The powder blast from the cartridge blackened his face, while the bullet completely mutilated the top of his head. In fact, some in the crowd suggested that the body may not have been Wellington's after all, but rather was another victim of the fugitive's escape effort. The body was not clothed in the canvas coat that Wellington had worn during his trial. On closer inspection, however, another miner announced that the body still had the remnants of a strange blue cloth cap that Wellington had worn that night. There was a murmur of agreement. Just like that, it was settled.

With that, not another thought was given to Wellington's body. It was now time to settle the matter of Hansen's fate. Someone in the crowd said, "Let's go back and hang Hansen!" Many others yelled their agreement. Off the men went, back to the saloon.

As things began to settle down, however, some miners seemed to have a change of heart. Perhaps Wellington's death played on the minds of the miners as they vacillated over Hansen's punishment. Eventually, after some debate, a consensus solution emerged. The young man from Sweden would not hang, but would rather endure the lash fifty times at noon the following day. Perhaps Wellington had made the right decision earlier that evening.

As the miners gathered in the late morning to carry out the sentence, a short and thin man volunteered to whip Hansen. The Swede cooperated as he was tied to the stump and his four flannel shirts were removed. The camp buzzed with anticipation as residents jockeyed for a good position to watch. Some climbed to the roofs of the few cabins in the vicinity while others took pictures of the event. One of the few women in the camp pushed her way through the crowd up to Hansen and asked him to look at her camera as she took his picture.

At that point, the crowd settled down and got quiet, for the small man with the whip had just stepped into the circle. He announced to the crowd that he did not enjoy the fact that he was about to inflict pain and misery on a convicted thief, but that he did it for the good of the camp and for law and order. He struck blows for honesty and justice in the camp and in the gold fields. With that, he raised the handle of the whip and let the lash fly with unexpected fury and speed.

Although he took the first few lashes well, as was mentioned above, every blow left purple stripes on the back of the hapless convicted thief. As Hansen became more demonstrative of the pain and suffering he endured, the frenzied man who held the whip seemed to increase the intensity and ferocity of his blows. The scene drew excitement from the crowd, and after about the fifteenth lash fell, there emerged a heated debate among the spectators. Some onlookers thought that the affair had gone far enough, while others screamed for blood.

One man in the crowd, a storekeeper in the camp, shouted for the man with the whip to pour it on the thief. A nearby miner shot a look of anger at the storekeeper and charged him with being a thief too. The storekeeper turned to the man and returned the accusation, calling him as much a thief as himself. The heated exchange actually led to both men drawing their handguns to take aim at each other. The crowd did not seem to miss a beat. Those men in either duelist's line of fire simply shifted position to achieve relative safety. It became confusing for some who could not decide which spectacle to watch.

Finally, a miner stepped in between the two and demanded that they put their weapons down. Both complied without further incident, secretly relieved, no doubt, that someone had intervened to prevent them from doing something they might have painfully or existentially regretted seconds later.

Meanwhile, back at the whipping post, Hansen was reduced to an exhausted whimper. The fanatic with the whip continued to lay it on Hansen's back with vigor. Finally, the Mizner brothers had had enough. Together, the four stepped in authoritatively and stated with finality that Hansen's ordeal was now completed. Nobody argued with the pronouncement. All in attendance had had their vengeance sated, save the man holding the whip. But as he calmed down from his frenzy, he too complied.

The miners gave Hansen his shirts and then fed him a large meal. He ate the food with apparent indifference to what he had just experienced. Then he lit his pipe, accepted the plaque that was draped around his neck with the word thief inscribed upon it, and made his way down the trail to Dyea. He knew that he could never show his face on the Chilkoot Trail again or he would be killed.

After Hansen walked out of view, the camp residents immediately set themselves to the task of trying to dig a shallow grave in the frozen ground for Wellington. It took some doing, but they finally laid his body in the ground and a preacher said a few words over him. It was an ironic little burial sermon, replete with the admonition that men who hoped to get rich quick will reap a just reward. Addison Mizner and others thought that this was a strange thing to say in front of a throng of gold rush stampeders.

Most men no doubt never gave the funeral service a moment's thought. There were golden riches waiting on the other side of the mountains, and they were burning daylight.

Jefferson Randolph "Soapy" Smith, the Dictator of Skagway

An icy cold winter day on the White Pass trail could leave a man curiously thirsty for a stiff drink. And so it was for Andy McGrath, a toll road employee on the White Pass, who made his way down the trail to Skagway for some weekend fun in January 1898. He stepped up to the bar, slapped his bill down, and called for a drink. The saloon keeper, John Fay, brought him a libation and took the money. Fay, however, did not return with any change. McGrath confronted Fay about the matter, whereupon Fay unceremoniously threw him out of the saloon. Not only did he not get his due change, but McGrath also lost the drink he had ordered. A man should not receive such treatment, he told the local deputy marshal, a man called Rowan.

After Rowan heard the complaint, he told McGrath that he needed to find the doctor for his wife, who had just gone into labor. The deputy walked with McGrath to the saloon, hoping to quickly resolve the dispute, and perhaps find a doctor at the same time. This was Skagway, after all. As the two men walked into the saloon, Fay met them with a hail of gunfire, cutting them down. Rowan and McGrath fell dying to the floor.

Skagway residents soon heard the news. Townsmen responded with an uproar. Fay felt the heat immediately and sought refuge with his gambling friends. These men claimed ties to the leader of the organized criminal underworld of

Skagway, a man called "Soapy" Smith. As mobs looked for Fay in the alleys, on the streets, and in the brothels and saloons, Smith put the word out on the streets that he commanded 200 gunmen in town. Anyone who tried to put a rope around Fay's neck would be shot, Smith warned.

Soapy Smith was no ordinary two-bit crime boss. He quickly moved to not only protect Fay, but also to enhance his personal reputation in town. He convinced Fay to surrender to the authorities, and then used his influence network to control the meeting called to administer justice. The men selected to guard, investigate, and serve as jurors were all Smith's men. Their names had been put forward by the editor of the local paper, the Skagway *Alaskan,* who also worked for Smith. Territorial officials eventually tried Fay in Sitka. He received a light sentence. Meanwhile, Smith milked the incident for all it was worth. He raised money to give to Rowan's widow and fatherless child, listing himself as the first contributor. Smith used the tragedy to appear as a defender of law and order, an enemy of mob justice, a benefactor to widows, a charitable businessman, and a man who could offer protection to criminals. Smith was at the top of his game, and he knew it; he was the self-proclaimed "Dictator of Skagway."

Jefferson Randolph Smith hailed from Georgia. Although no documentation exists to prove it, he claimed to be a member of a prominent Southern family. He had the ability to turn on the Southern charm and genteel behavior. Smith used these attributes to con people everywhere he set up shop. His smooth Southern drawl, highbrow turn of phrase, and calls to honor and chivalrous behavior proved irresistible. Perhaps his powers of persuasion were honed when he studied to be a Baptist preacher.

Smith left his wife and six children in St. Louis to embark on a famously checkered career. He soon achieved success as a crime boss through hard work and determination. Who knows what heights Smith might have scaled in the legitimate business world had he only loosed his endless energy and talent on legal pursuits. Smith traveled in powerful circles and knew many connected people. He carried on a substantial correspondence with many politicians, civic leaders, and powerful citizens in both North and South America.

Smith began his career as an underworld figure in Leadville, Colorado. He first arrived in that town from Texas, where he hired on to herd cattle on the famous Chisholm Trail. While in Leadville a man called Taylor befriended him and taught him most of the tricks of the bunko trade, including the shell game, and how to make a deck of cards work for you. He took these lessons and mastered them, even adding a few phrases to the American lexicon, including the "sure-thing game." Smith eventually ended up in Denver, where he exerted an extensive influence on organized criminal activity. He had his hands in all types of con and bunko operations and became known as "Soapy." (In his early con man years, he would set up a table with soap bars on it. He would then wrap bills of various denominations around the soap, followed by a white wrapper. He'd mix the bars up and offer to sell them for one dollar. He had a shill in the crowd who bought the bar containing the hundred dollar bill, at which point this whipped up the interest of the onlookers who would then buy the soap bars. Smith knew which bars had bills and which did not, and

JefferJeffersonJefferson Randolph "Soapy" Smith, the Dictator of Skagway

it subsequently became a famous con game and earned him the name "Soapy.") Even local barbers were in on his network. They customarily nicked the necks of wealthy men to signal Soapy's associates that they were good marks for a fleecing.

From Denver, Smith moved on to a silver mining camp called Creede, also in Colorado. He moved his entire operation there and pushed out other small-time con men that refused to function under his control. After the silver boom died out in Creede, Smith returned to Denver until 1897. In that year the first news about the Klondike strike in Canada hit the presses. The entrepreneurial Smith knew that this gold strike presented unique opportunities, but they would only last for a short time. He needed to act before the early birds and law-and-order types established control of the region. Smith wanted to be in on the ground floor to take full advantage of the opportunities presented by the disorder of a gold rush.

This operation was to be the crown jewel of his outlaw career. Smith wanted to gain control over a boomtown—not just its underworld, but the entire town. This plan called for accomplices, and he handpicked associates based on their years of service, loyalty, and skill sets. There was the "Reverend" Charles Bowers, a longtime associate who possessed a voice like a preacher and an appearance of calm and piety that allowed him to pull off his deceptions with a flawless panache. But this peaceful facade hid a ruthless reality. Bowers had committed cold-blooded murders, including the time that he had shot and killed a policeman. Smith wanted Bowers because of his solid ability to steer new suckers to the phony businesses run by associates where they would be quickly separated from their money. Smith also respected his knowledge of secret handshakes and signals used by fraternal societies. Use of these coded communications allowed him to disarm even the most cautious victims.

Then there was Syd Dixon, the son of an extremely wealthy family who had been raised in exclusive social circles. Well educated and sophisticated, Dixon carried himself with an aristocratic air so convincing that he was able to gain the confidence of men of means and distinction. He resorted to a life of crime because he had squandered his portion of the family fortune on an opium addiction, and was desperate to maintain his drug habit and playboy lifestyle.

George Wilder served the Smith gang as its advance man. He played the role of a successful businessman with an insider's knowledge of a sure-thing deal. He could quickly gain the confidence of strangers and convince them that he had a great investment opportunity.

A few other men who served as muscle and intelligence gatherers rounded out the well-seasoned company of scoundrels. They invaded Southeast Alaska as if engaged in a military operation. First, they scouted out potential sites to locate their base of operations. Skagway eventually emerged as the chosen site; it was perfect in Smith's view because it would be the main point of entry into the Klondike. And, there was almost no law and order present in the entire region. Territorial officials commissioned only a U.S. marshal and one deputy to serve the entire Alaskan panhandle.

The Soapy Smith gang hit Skagway in 1897 like a tidal wave. By October, a matter of weeks after arrival, the gang took over control of the town's underworld. They ran con games, illegitimate business establishments, rigged gambling tables, shell games, and street thefts. Meanwhile, the leader of the gang maintained the aura of upstanding citizen and supporter of law and order. Smith never missed an opportunity to appear on the side of legal authorities. He wore conservative business attire, spoke in a soft and educated manner, and established a social network of legitimate town leaders that included journalists, clergy, and businessmen. He was known to attend Bible classes, even occasionally teaching a session. Smith even raised funds for the church and for the indigent, and he passed out $20 bills to the widowed and homeless at Christmastime.

On a voyage from Seattle to Skagway aboard the steamship *City of Seattle,* Smith saw an accident occur that killed a passenger. The drunk victim had been swinging from a hanging light fixture that broke loose from the ceiling and crashed down onto his head, crushing his skull. The vessel was overcrowded and passengers were already predisposed against the ship's captain for the unpleasant conditions. They decided to make an issue of the accident and called a meeting which resulted in a resolution to sue the shipping company for $50,000 in damages.

Smith saw his chance and took it. He rifled through the pockets of the dead man and produced an item that he claimed was his. He accused the deceased of being a thief and challenged the leaders of the meeting to continue to press their case against the shipping company in the name of the dead man, whom Smith described as a "cheat" and a "bum." This had the desired effect, cementing his reputation among the passengers as a man who championed law and order. The incident also prevented the passengers from taking over the vessel and demanding its return to Seattle where they wanted to press their case. In short order, the ship disgorged its angry but subdued passengers in Skagway. There, Smith and his men set about to fleece as many of them as they could get their hooks into.

By early spring a conflict for the heart and soul of Skagway raged. It pitted law-abiding folk against the operators of saloons and gambling houses and con games. Smith emerged as the leading figure of the latter. Another early arrival to the Skagway scene, a man called Frank Reid, spoke on behalf of the former. The middle-aged Reid had been one of the first men to arrive on the beach at Skagway. He had helped to lay out the town site, and possessed impeccable credentials as a Western pioneer. Reid hailed from Illinois and had received a degree from the University of Michigan. He had trekked across the plains, fought Indians in Oregon, become a schoolteacher in the Willamette Valley, and then had headed to the Far North to seek his fortune in the Klondike rush. He earned a reputation as a fearless man, a good engineer and surveyor, and a dead aim with a gun. Even Soapy Smith begrudgingly respected and, some said, feared Reid.

Along with two former policemen friends, Reid organized a vigilance committee in the wake of the crime spree touched off by Smith's gang and associated outlaws. The committee called on the federal government to send troops and place the town under martial law. The troops arrived on February 8, 1898. With this backing, the vigilantes made a move to clean out Skagway of its undesirable elements. Most of the underworld figures either left town on their own to ply their schemes in other Alaskan locations (at least until the heat died down), or the committee drove them out. Most, that is, except for Soapy Smith himself. So successful had he been at cultivating a reputation of supporting law and order that many members of the vigilance committee believed he was a good and public-spirited man.

The accomplishments of the vigilantes proved to be fleeting. Smith sent most of his gang and associates away until the storm unleashed by the vigilantes had passed. They continued to rob and con stampeders on the trails and in other camps and gold towns. Soapy Smith continued to get his cut from these activities. Holdups and shootings became more frequent outside of town, and within a matter of weeks the lawless element began to drift back into Skagway. By this time, Smith was in full control of the criminal element in the community.

By early March, it seemed that the situation had grown worse than ever. The vigilance committee met again and posted a warning:

> WARNING
> A Word to the Wise should be sufficient. All con
> men, bunco and sure-thing men and all other
> objectionable characters are notified to leave Skagway
> and the White Pass Road immediately and remain
> away. Failure to comply with this warning will be
> followed by prompt action.
>   Signed: The Committee of 101 [term used to
> demonstrate the strength in numbers of the committee]

Rather than allow such an announcement to scare him, Smith calmly responded with subterfuge to confuse the situation. He formed his own vigilance committee, called the Committee of Law and Order. Smith moved to win over the legitimate business community to his side by presenting himself as the rightful representative of the law in Skagway. He divided the town into newcomers and established commercial interests, and warned the latter that the former had created the current troubles in order to gain economic control of the town. This charge stretched the bounds of credulity. Frank Reid, after all, had been in Skagway almost from the day it was founded, and his friends ran the initial businesses in the community. But, it was a credit to Smith's abilities of persuasion that he successfully implemented this bit of propaganda.

Smith put up posters all over town with a warning of his own:

> The business interests of Skagway propose to put
> a stop to the lawless acts of many newcomers. We
> hereby summon all good citizens to a meeting at which
> these matters will be discussed. Come one, come all!
> Immediate action will be taken for relief. Let this be a
> warning to those cheechakos [newcomers to Alaska]
> who are disgracing our city. The meeting will be held at
> Sylvester Hall at 8 p.m. sharp.
> Signed: Jefferson R. Smith, Chairman

Smith led a rousing meeting that night, pledging to devote his life to the protection of the residents of Skagway. The crowd greeted the speech enthusiastically. Strategically placed members of the Smith gang helped to whip up the frenzy of support for their leader. Smith's committee posted another proclamation stating that 317 men stood ready to respond to any action that they believed smacked of vigilantism or blackmail.

The strategy worked. Smith successfully divided and confused Skagway residents. He further complicated matters when some of his men infiltrated the rival Committee of 101. Gang members disrupted these meetings and created an air of fear, doubt, and disorder. The effort to clean up Skagway died out

Soapy Smith posing for a photograph in his saloon in Skagway, Alaska, in February 1898. *Alaska State Library, Wickersham State Historic Site Photographs, P277-001-009.*

and the troops returned to their post at Dyea. A triumphant Smith reassumed control of the town.

By April 1898, the Smith gang included in its ranks a motley crew of thugs, thieves, con men, prostitutes, gamblers, pimps, and so on. Many were closely tied to Smith, while others simply sought out his protection and a little turf to operate their own illegal activities in exchange for a percentage. Above them all, Smith continued to portray himself as an upstanding and law-abiding town booster and father.

Smith lived by and enforced a rule within his network to never go after a full-time resident of Skagway. He even went so far as to return money to a young chief of the Skagway fire department after members of his organization robbed him.

He returned the money and then trashed the men responsible for the deed. Smith occasionally staged events in which he prevented minor larcenies in public to bolster his image. These were so successful that even worried parents sought Smith's help to track down their wayward daughters. Smith also took the part of the local stevedores when they went on strike. This stance earned him the support of organized labor in Skagway. He also endeared himself to local church ministers by leading donation drives. Smith even curried public favor by leading a well-publicized campaign to adopt the stray dogs of Skagway.

While these activities appeared to be self-serving, the kingpin of Skagway developed into a complex figure that used much of his ill-gotten gains for philanthropic purposes. Indeed, despite the vast and profitable crime network that he ran, he possessed almost no personal capital or assets. For example, Smith set up a widows' fund. Oftentimes the women who received money from Smith had been made widows by Smith's own men. He provided support for men who had become paupers while in the Klondike, including men who had lost everything to Smith's crime network. Smith paid for the funerals of people who died with no money and no friends.

Such generosity paid dividends, of course. It seemed that Smith had all the major community institutions under his sway in one way or another. He had a tough group of skilled men plying their nefarious trades and bringing him his 50 percent cut. He had a broad spy network within Skagway and along the trails, sending in intelligence regarding potential victims to be fleeced and the disposition of community members and authorities. He had a team of men organizing and analyzing the data that his spies sent in. Finally, he possessed an uncanny ability to influence public perception.

By the summer of 1898, Soapy Smith appeared to reach the pinnacle of his power. He presided over a well-oiled criminal machine that reached into the Pacific Northwest states and beyond, into Central America. The criminal mastermind even led the Fourth of July parade through town and then sat next to the Territorial governor on a rostrum draped with flags. In public, he appeared as the fair-minded proprietor of the best restaurant in Skagway, an oyster bar that served up the most sumptuous meals available in town. It was located in the center of Skagway's business district and had a beautiful bar made of imported mahogany. This facade, like the owner's public image, served as a screen to hide a dark underside. Behind the mahogany bar, there was a smaller parlor where Smith's nefarious associates bilked many a bright-eyed and trusting cheechako of all their money. Outside of the small parlor was a high-fenced outside yard fitted with a secret passage that allowed Smith's associates to flee without a trace. Then, once the victim realized the game that he had fallen for and gave chase, he would be dumbfounded by the empty fenced yard.

All of the ill-gotten gains for this plot went into Smith's safe, but he always stayed out of it personally. Occasionally he tried to help out a poor wayfaring victim and adopted the pretense of a great persuader of the outlaw element. He appeared to use his benevolent influence to get the thieves to return at least a portion of the loot to the victim. Smith, however, always got his 50 percent cut. He could legitimately claim that he had high expenses and took a big risk. There were bribes to dole out, attorneys to pay, and the need to silence the occasionally loud complaints from some who protested the treatment that they received in the parlor. The musclemen needed to eat too.

It was an incredible organization—or so it seemed. And yet the whole thing came crashing down after one man challenged Smith and refused to be cowed. J. D. Stewart prospected on the Yukon near Dawson in the Canadian Territory. He was not an especially bright man; in fact, to Smith's gang, he appeared ripe for the taking. Stewart came down from Dawson across the White Pass early that season to make his way back to British Columbia, where he intended to spend some of his hard-earned $2,800 in gold dust. His arrival signaled good things to come for many permanent residents in Skagway. Every year Skagway commercial interests eagerly awaited the exodus of gold-laden prospectors from the Klondike. Anxious to return home, many of these prospectors took the all-river route down the Yukon and out of Alaska by steamer through St. Michael. Although it was a much easier route, it took longer. Many chose to hike out in the mid- to late summer, down to either Skagway or Dyea. The business owners of both towns looked forward to the money that would be made from these men.

In the summer of 1898, Stewart made it to Skagway, where residents warned him to steer clear of Soapy Smith's oyster bar and saloon. Smith's men nevertheless talked him into entering the back parlor to weigh his gold for exchange by an assaying company. Sure enough, Stewart handed over the gold. Before he knew what had happened, it was on its way into the backyard. He tried to give chase, but Smith's men grabbed him and pretended that he was an out-of-control drunk. They pushed him through the saloon and out the front door onto the boardwalk. When he freed himself, he tried to find the man who had run off with his poke, but found nothing.

Stewart was fleeced and angry. He went straight to the local deputy marshal and demanded the return of his gold. The marshal, under the pay of Smith, told him that he could do nothing to help Stewart. He told Stewart that he should go back to the Klondike if wanted to get more gold.

This treatment did not sit well with Stewart, and he made his way through the community spreading news of what had happened. The town quickly was in an uproar. What would happen if news got out on the trail about this incident? Would all of the prospectors choose to take the Yukon route and avoid Skagway? This was a serious situation indeed.

By mid-day on July 8, Frank Reid and his two friends had re-formed the Committee of 101 to address the situation. Stewart's fleecing had become the only topic in town, and longtime residents had taken to the streets. The situation in Skagway grew tense as rumors circulated that Dawson's gold miners were all choosing to take the Yukon River route out of the Klondike. The townspeople, who had cheered Soapy Smith at the Fourth of July festivities just a few days before, now cursed his name.

Smith's spies worked overtime to gather information about the tenor of the community. They told him that a crowd had gathered outside the storefront of a local outfitter. Smith donned his mackinaw coat, shoved his revolvers into the large front pockets, and walked down to confront them. When he arrived he castigated them for cowardice and dared them to challenge him. They could see the outlines of the handguns in his coat. The crowd melted away and Smith returned to his restaurant.

Soon afterward, Judge Sehlbrede from Dyea arrived. He met with Smith and suggested that it might be wise to assist in the return of Stewart's gold. It would go a long way toward resolving the situation and defusing the tension. Smith angrily retorted that Stewart had lost his money fair and square through gambling, but that he would see what he could do. The judge told Smith that he would give him until four o'clock that afternoon to facilitate the return of the gold, or else . . .

The entire town had turned against Smith. None of his gang or associates had ever experienced anything quite like this turn of events. Fear gripped them. Some of his confidants saw the writing on the wall and urged him to cooperate. Many others in the crime syndicate lost their composure. A good many quietly slipped out of town.

The combination of the townsfolk and his own gang turning against him made Smith stubbornly dig in his heels. To back down now would ruin everything he had worked so hard to build. He would suffer a loss of face publicly. It would end his ability to run the town and his illicit operation. Soapy Smith had become egomaniacal. Who were these people to tell him what to do or to make threats and demands? He started to drink that afternoon. Soapy rarely touched the stuff. This resort to the bottle suggested that the stress of the situation was playing heavily on his nerves. The booze also dulled his ability to think rationally.

As the afternoon wore on and the deadline came and went, Smith continued to hit the bottle. It sustained his cocksure attitude, but something was different about the source of his courage and bluster. Before it had been genuine, but now, in the face of this, his most intense crisis, it seemed to his close associates that for the first time Soapy did not know what to do. Smith had taken to the street outside his restaurant where he paced back and forth with a rifle in his hand. He swore out oaths of vengeance to those that sought to harm him. The man who had ruled Skagway with the velvet glove covering the iron fist stood exposed for what he was: a violent thug and criminal.

By nine o'clock that evening, the drink and strain finally got to Smith. He started to walk alone down the deserted streets of Skagway, still with his rifle in hand. Twilight descended on the quiet town as Smith made his way down to the docks. A small crowd began to gather behind him, keeping a wary distance. Smith noticed the men following him and derided them as cowards. He dared them to come closer and then demanded that they go home. None accepted his challenges, but none of them went home, either.

At the docks, Frank Reid stood with three other men. They guarded the gangway that led to the location of a vigilance committee meeting. As Smith turned a corner near the docks, about twelve of his men fell into formation behind him. It was a scene meant for Hollywood. The gang continued relentlessly toward certain trouble.

As they drew near the docks, Smith and his entourage by chance ran into John Clancy, one of Smith's partners in the restaurant. Clancy warned Smith that if wanted to stay alive, he better turn around. Smith brushed him aside with a wave of his Colt .45 revolver. Clancy told Smith to suit himself and walked back into town.

As Smith neared the ramp to the dock, Reid spotted him. He told Smith that he would not be allowed to disrupt the meeting, and to back off. "Damn you, Reid," Smith retorted.

"You're at the bottom of all my troubles. I should have got rid of you three months ago." Smith continued until the two adversaries stood face-to-face, neither willing to back down from the challenger. It was a moment that would have inspired a filmmaker such as Sergio Leone, who famously dramatized his spaghetti Westerns with extreme close-ups of gunfighters about to swing into action.

The two men continued to stare each other down. Suddenly, Smith raised his Winchester lever-action rifle and pointed the barrel at Reid's head. Reid responded instantly by grabbing the muzzle and forcing it down toward the ground, while at the same time reaching for his holstered revolver with the other hand. Reid now had the drop on Smith, who, panic-stricken, pleaded with Reid not to shoot. But it was too late. Reid pulled the trigger. Misfire! At that moment, Smith's rifle went off and a bullet shattered Reid's hip. Reid fell to the ground, but kept his wits about him and squeezed the trigger again just as Smith fired a second time. This time Reid's gun fired. Although Smith's second shot tore into Reid's leg, Reid's aim was true. His second shot tore through Smith's heart. The dictator of Skagway fell, dying. Reid fired a third round and hit Smith in the knee as he crumpled to the ground.

The two men lay in a pool of blood. Smith gasped once more for air and then became motionless. Reid was writhing in agony, mortally wounded. A woman screamed nearby. Reid's compatriots rushed to his assistance and raised their guns menacingly at the Smith gang. Smith's men looked at their fallen leader and then at each other. Slowly they started to back away from the scene as a mob of vigilantes began to make haste in an effort to support their wounded hero.

As they reached Reid, the bleeding man, in agony, managed to say, "I'm badly hurt, boys, but I got him first." The vigilantes gave Reid three cheers as they placed him on a stretcher. Then they followed him as he was whisked off to see a doctor. Smith's body lay all night where it fell.

In the aftermath, Reid died of his wounds. The good people of Skagway buried both Reid and Smith in the community cemetery. Reid's funeral was the largest in Skagway history, and the town placed a large monument at his grave that attested to his bravery. It read: HE GAVE HIS LIFE FOR THE HONOR OF SKAGWAY.

U.S. and Canadian officials tracked down members of Smith's gang. There was no escape from Skagway. The authorities closed down the dock with a dragnet. The Canadian Mounties guarded the passes into the Klondike. There was nowhere to run and no place to hide. One by one the gang members were either captured or turned themselves in. Law and order finally came to Skagway.

Bibliography

Charles Hendrickson: The Blue Parka Bandit

H.C. Landru. *The Blue Parka Man: Alaskan Gold Rush Bandit*. New York: Dodd, Mead, & Co., 1980.

The Discoverer

William, Ogilvie. *Early Days on the Yukon & The Story of Its Gold Finds*. London: John Lane, the Bodley Head, 1913.

Fred Hardy

Ferrell, Ed. *Frontier Justice*. Bowie, MD: Heritage Books, 1998.

Green, Melissa S. "A History of the Death Penalty in Alaska," University of Alaska Anchorage Justice Center Web Site, rev. 21 September 2001, http://justice.uaa.alaska.edu/death/alaska/history.html.

Hardy, Fred, Plff. in Err., v. United States. http://openjurist .org/186.

September 19, 1902, *Nome Nugget*.

Klutuk: "The Man from the Mountain"

Bell, Tom. "Memories of a Murder," *Alaska Magazine*, October 1991.

Bibliography

Ferrell, Ed. *Frontier Justice*, 98–102.

Hatfield, Fred. *North of the Sun: A Memoir of the Alaskan Wilderness*. New York: Birch Lane Press Book, 1990.

———. "Of Traps and Treasures—Klutuk," *Alaska Magazine*, September 1984.

Ed Krause

Barkdull, Calvin H. "The Murder Gang," *The Alaska Sportsman* XXII (January 1956, no.1): 6–9, 26–29.

"Edward Krause, Under Sentence of Death for Murder of Captain Plunkett, Escapes from Prison," *The Daily Alaska Dispatch*, Juneau, Alaska, 13 April 1917, page 1.

Hunt, William R. *Distant Justice: Policing the Alaska Frontier*. Norman, OK: University of Oklahoma Press, 1987.

"Will Krause Secrets Ever Be Known?" *The Daily Alaska Dispatch*, Juneau, Alaska, 17 April 1917, page 1.

William "Slim" Birch

Ferrell, Ed. *Frontier Justice*.

The Juneau *Mining Record*, 27 January 1897 and 3 February 1897.

Wilbanks, William. *Forgotten Heroes: Police Officers Killed in Alaska, 1850–1897*. Nashville, TN: Turner Publishing, 1999.

Bibliography

Nellie "Black Bear" Bates and William Schermeyer

Butler, Anne M. *Daughters of Joy, Sisters of Misery: Prostitutes in the American West, 1865–90.* Champaign: University of Illinois Press, 1987.

Hunt, William R. *Distant Justice.*

Murphy, Claire Rudolf, and Jane G. Haigh. *Gold Rush Women.* Anchorage: Alaska Northwest Books, 2003.

Thomas Johnson: The Blueberry Kid

Bleakley, Geoffrey T. "Murder on the Koyukuk: The Hunt for the Blueberry Kid," *Alaska History* 11, no. 1, Spring 1996.

Hunt, William R. *Distant Justice.*

Joe Horner, aka Frank Canton

Dale, Edward Everett, ed. *Frontier Trails: The Autobiography of Frank Canton.* Boston and New York: Houghton Mifflin, 1930.

Hunt, William R. *Distant Justice.*

George O'Brien

Ferrell, Ed. *Frontier Justice.*

Reid, Leo. *Dawson Daily News,* 9 June 1911.

Bibliography

The Sheep Camp Vigilantes of Chilkoot Pass

Berton, Pierre. *Klondike: The Life and Death of the Last Great Gold Rush.* Toronto: McClelland & Stewart Ltd, 1963.

Hunt, William R. *Distant Justice.*

White, E. J. "Stroller," *Stroller's Weekly,* 20 November 1930.

Jefferson Randolph "Soapy" Smith, the Dictator of Skagway

Berton, Pierre. *Klondike.*

Index

Index

Index

Index

Index

Index

Wellington, William, 154, 159–67

White, Tommy, 10

Wilder, George, 174

Wiseman, Frank, 14–17, 49–52

women in Alaska, 92–94

Y

Yamamoto, Kato, 69

About the Author

John W. Heaton is an associate professor of history at the University of Alaska Fairbanks. As a graduate student he specialized in American Indian history and the History of the American West, and earned an MA from Utah State University and a PhD from Arizona State University. He has lived in Fairbanks since 2000 and now considers himself an expert on snow, subfreezing temperatures, winter darkness, and changing flat tires at 40 below. He is the author of *The Shoshone-Bannocks: Culture and Commerce at Fort Hall, 1870–1940*, and scholarly articles on Native Americans. His current project focuses on the history of Athabascan communities in the Alaskan Interior.